Harmony in the Wild

Harmony in the Wild

A Global Approach to Tiger Conservation

Sanyub S.

UNIEK ENTERPRISES

CONTENTS

INDEX

Introduction

Chapter 6 Legal Frameworks and Policies
6.1 International Agreements for Tiger Protection
6.2National Legislation Supporting Conservation
6.3Challenges and Opportunities in Enforcing Conservation Laws

Chapter 7 Economic Considerations and Conservation Financing
7.1 Economic Benefits of Tiger Conservation
7.2Funding Models for Sustainable Conservation Efforts
7.3Public-Private Partnerships in Tiger Protection

Chapter 8Education and Awareness
8.1Importance of Public Awareness in Conservation
8.2Educational Programs for Communities and Schools
8.3Media and Its Role in Advocating for Tiger Conservation

Chapter 9 Challenges and Future Outlook
9.1Ongoing Threats to Tiger Populations
9.2Anticipated Challenges in Global Conservation Efforts
9.3 Strategies for Building a Sustainable Future for Tigers

In the core of the 21st 100 years, mankind faces an exceptional test: the sensitive harmony among improvement and natural protection. No place is this battle more obvious than in the destiny of the world's famous huge feline, the tiger. Once going generally across Asia, the tiger has seen its living spaces psychologist and populaces decline radically because of human exercises, environment misfortune, and poaching. Because of this basic crossroads, an aggressive and extraordinary drive has arisen - "Congruity in Nature: A Worldwide Way to deal with Tiger Preservation."

The Beginning of Agreement: A Dire Source of inspiration

As we stand observer to the disturbing decrease in tiger numbers, "Concordance in Nature" isn't just a reaction; it is a resonating source of inspiration. Conceived out of an aggregate acknowledgment that the endurance of the tiger rises above borders, this worldwide methodology unites countries, hippies, researchers, and neighborhood networks under a typical flag. The beginning of this drive lies in recognizing that the protection of tigers requests a change in outlook - a shift towards cooperative, cross-line endeavors that address both the quick dangers and the main drivers of the emergency.

The Worldwide Tiger Emergency: Figuring out the Desperation

Prior to diving into the complexities of "Congruity in the Wild," getting a handle on the seriousness of the worldwide tiger crisis is pivotal. Generally worshipped and representing strength and elegance, tigers currently wind up helpless before human development. Fast urbanization, deforestation, and unlawful untamed life exchange have devastated their natural surroundings, driving these magnificent animals to the edge of annihilation. The earnestness of the circumstance requires a unified front - a worldwide partnership focused on protecting the wild scenes that tigers call home.

An All encompassing Methodology: Past Limits and Boundaries

At its center, "Concordance in Nature" epitomizes a comprehensive methodology that reaches out past geological limits and regulatory boundaries. Perceiving that environments are interconnected and that the endurance of tigers is dependent upon the prosperity of their territories, this drive reclassifies protection systems. It isn't simply about safeguarding tigers yet about cultivating concordance between human turn of events and natural life protection. By tending to the underlying drivers of the emergency and coordinating maintainable practices, "Congruity in Nature" expects to make a reality where people and tigers coincide amicably.

Custom fitted Answers for Different Scenes

One of the characterizing elements of "Congruity in Nature" is its obligation to custom fitted answers for the different scenes that tigers possess. From the thick mangrove woods of the Sundarbans to the huge taiga of Siberia, every area presents special difficulties that require tweaked protection draws near. Drawing on state of the art advances, logical ability, and the insight of nearby networks, this worldwide drive explores the intricacies of differed biological systems, guaranteeing that protection procedures are viable, socially delicate, and practical.

Coordinated effort as the Foundation: A Call for Worldwide Solidarity

Cooperation lies at the core of "Concordance in the Wild." The drive perceives that the preservation of tigers isn't the obligation of a solitary country however a common responsibility that traverses borders. Legislatures, NGOs, scientists, and networks from different corners of the globe meet up under a shared objective: to get a future where tigers flourish in nature. The call for worldwide solidarity reverberations through the passageways of force, moving countries to save contrasts for a common regular legacy.

Local area Commitment: Enabling Those at the Bleeding edges

In the terrific embroidered artwork of tiger preservation, nearby networks arise as pivotal partners. "Amicability in Nature" puts huge accentuation on local area commitment, understanding that the progress of any preservation exertion relies on the help and contribution of the people who live close by these grand animals. Through mindfulness programs, training drives, and the coordination of economical practices, the drive means to enable networks to become stewards of their regular environmental factors, cultivating a feeling of shared liability regarding the prosperity of the two people and tigers.

Mechanical Developments: Exploring the Outskirts of Protection

As we set out on this aggressive excursion, "Amicability in Nature" use the force of mechanical advancements to explore the wildernesses of protection. Satellite following, information examination, and man-made brainpower become essential apparatuses in observing tiger developments, surveying environment wellbeing, and recognizing possible dangers. The marriage of state of the art science and customary environmental information prepares for another period in tiger preservation, where accuracy and versatility are critical to progress.

The Vision Ahead: An Existence Where Tigers Wander Indiscriminately

All things considered, the vision set out by "Congruity in Nature" is one of trust and assurance. It is a dream where the sound of stirring leaves and the thunder of a tiger reverberation through scenes pure by the infringement of human advancement.

It is a dream of a reality where tigers meander indiscriminately, filling in as signs of ecological wellbeing and images of our common obligation to agreeable concurrence. This presentation fills in as an entry into the many-sided embroidery of "Congruity in the Wild," welcoming perusers to investigate the complex layers of a worldwide drive ready to shape the predetermination of quite possibly of Earth's most loved specie.

1. **Overview of the Current State of Tiger Conservation**

   The magnificent tiger, once venerated across societies for its solidarity and magnificence, presently faces an existential danger that requests dire consideration. The present status of tiger preservation is a mind boggling scene of difficulties, progress, and the tenacious battle to get a future for this notorious species.

   The Test: An Animal types on the Edge

   As of the most recent evaluations, worldwide tiger populaces are at a basic point. The Worldwide Association for Protection of Nature (IUCN) Red Rundown classifies a few tiger subspecies as jeopardized or fundamentally imperiled. Environment misfortune because of human exercises, uncontrolled poaching driven by the unlawful natural life exchange, and human-untamed life struggle are among the essential elements driving these brilliant animals to the edge of elimination.

   Living space Misfortune and Fracture:

   Perhaps of the most squeezing challenge confronting tiger preservation is the tenacious misfortune and fracture of their regular territories. As human populaces grow, backwoods are cleared for agribusiness, logging, and foundation improvement. This infringement not just lessens the accessible living space for tigers yet in addition disturbs the complicated equilibrium of environments they depend on.

   Poaching and Unlawful Natural life Exchange:

   Poaching stays a grave concern, energized by the interest for tiger parts in customary medication and the colorful pet exchange. In spite of global endeavors to control unlawful untamed life exchange, tigers keep on being focused on for their skins, bones, and other body parts. The rewarding idea of this exchange represents a consistent danger to wild tiger populaces, especially in locales where policing tested by restricted assets and debasement.

   Human-Natural life Struggle:

   As human populaces venture into tiger domains, clashes unavoidably emerge. Tigers might go after domesticated animals, prompting reprisal from neighborhood networks.

   This pattern of contention further imperils tigers as retaliatory killings and natural surroundings corruption escalate. Powerful systems to alleviate human-untamed life struggle are imperative for the conjunction of networks and tigers.

   Progress in Tiger Preservation: A Promising sign

In the midst of the difficulties, there have been remarkable triumphs in tiger protection, showing the way that coordinated endeavors can have an effect.

Worldwide Drives:

Global coordinated efforts and drives play had a crucial impact in tending to the transboundary idea of tiger protection. The Worldwide Tiger Drive, sent off in 2010, united state run administrations, NGOs, and global associations with the aggressive objective of multiplying the wild tiger populace by 2022, the Chinese Year of the Tiger. While this particular objective might not have been met, the drive has catalyzed worldwide consideration and obligation to tiger protection.

Safeguarded Regions and Hall Advancement:

The foundation and powerful administration of safeguarded regions stay key to tiger preservation. These regions act as safe-havens where tigers can flourish undisturbed. Moreover, the making of natural life hallways interfacing divided living spaces has earned respect as a fundamental procedure. Passageways work with the development of tigers between segregated regions, advancing hereditary variety and decreasing the dangers related with inbreeding.

Local area Association:

Perceiving the essential job of neighborhood networks in tiger protection, numerous drives currently focus on local area commitment. Programs that give financial options in contrast to networks living close to tiger territories, combined with training on concurrence techniques, have shown promising outcomes. At the point when neighborhood networks become stewards of their normal environmental factors, the possibilities of effective preservation increment.

Mechanical Developments:

Progressions in innovation have reformed the field of tiger preservation. Camera traps, satellite following, and DNA examination contribute pivotal information for checking tiger populaces and grasping their way of behaving. Man-made reasoning and AI calculations are being utilized to dissect immense datasets, giving bits of knowledge that guide in preservation arranging and authorization.

The Street Ahead: Techniques for Future Achievement

While progress has been made, the street ahead is loaded with difficulties that request versatile and imaginative procedures.

Fortifying Legitimate Systems:

Compelling protection requires powerful lawful structures that discourage poaching and environment obliteration. Fortifying and authorizing untamed life security regulations, both at public and worldwide levels, is fundamental. Moreover, tending to the interest for tiger items through severe punishments and public mindfulness crusades is urgent to checking unlawful exchange.

Putting resources into Against Poaching Endeavors:

Combatting poaching requires huge interests in enemy of poaching measures. This incorporates the preparation and preparing of natural life implementation groups, the utilization of innovation for observation, and global collaboration to destroy the crook networks behind unlawful natural life exchange.

Reasonable Improvement Practices:

Advancing reasonable improvement rehearses that balance the requirements of networks with preservation objectives is foremost. This includes incorporating preservation into land-use arranging, taking on eco-accommodating farming practices, and advancing dependable the travel industry that limits its effect on tiger environments.

Environmental Change Flexibility:

Environmental change represents an extra test to tiger preservation. Increasing temperatures, changing precipitation examples, and more incessant outrageous climate occasions can influence both tiger natural surroundings and prey accessibility. Protection procedures should integrate environmental change strength to guarantee the drawn out endurance of tiger populaces.

Public Mindfulness and Schooling:

A very much educated public is a strong partner in the battle for tiger protection. Instructive projects that bring issues to light about the significance of tigers in environments, the dangers they face, and the job of people in preservation endeavors can cultivate a feeling of obligation and collect help for defensive measures.

Transboundary Collaboration:

Tigers don't perceive political lines, and their protection requires cooperative endeavors across nations. Reinforcing transboundary participation, sharing knowledge on natural life wrongdoing, and blending preservation procedures are fundamental for the progress of worldwide drives.

2. **Importance of Global Collaboration in Preserving Tiger Species**

In the multifaceted embroidered artwork of Earth's biodiversity, not many animals order as much amazement and adoration as the tiger. Representing strength, excellence, and untamed wild, these magnificent large felines face an existential danger that rises above public boundaries. As we explore the Anthropocene, set apart by human strength and natural change, the significance of worldwide cooperation in protecting tiger species turns out to be progressively obvious. This paper investigates the diverse components of this objective, looking at the difficulties looked by tigers, the biological meaning of their conservation, and the job of brought together worldwide endeavors in getting their future.

The Tiger's Predicament: Difficulties Across Lines

Tigers and Natural surroundings Misfortune:

Tigers, with their tremendous home reaches and regional way of behaving, are especially defenseless against environment misfortune. As human populaces extend, timberlands are cleared for farming, framework advancement, and urbanization, bringing about the fracture and debasement of tiger environments. This challenge knows no limits; it traverses mainlands and requires global collaboration to address the underlying drivers.

Unlawful Untamed life Exchange and Transnational Organizations:
The unlawful untamed life exchange, driven by interest for tiger parts in conventional medication and extravagance products, works as a worldwide organization that takes advantage of permeable lines. Criminal associations participate in poaching, dealing, and sneaking, making it basic for countries to team up in destroying these organizations. A unified front is fundamental to reinforce policing, lawful systems, and battle the transnational idea of this unlawful exchange.

Human-Untamed life Struggle in Shared Scenes:
In areas where tigers and human populaces share scenes, clashes unavoidably emerge. As human settlements infringe upon customary tiger regions, conflicts happen over assets, prompting retaliatory killings and living space corruption. Relieving human-untamed life struggle requires composed endeavors, shared information, and the improvement of techniques that oblige both human necessities and the preservation of tiger populaces.

The Natural Meaning of Tigers: Past Magnetic Megafauna

Tigers as Umbrella Species:
Past their charming allure, tigers assume a pivotal part as an umbrella species. Safeguarding tiger environments frequently involves protecting huge, biodiverse scenes that help a heap of animal varieties. By defending tigers, we coincidentally shield the whole environment, from dominant hunters to the littlest life forms, guaranteeing the biological equilibrium of these scenes.

Managing Prey Populaces:
Tigers go about as controllers of prey populaces, forestalling overgrazing and keeping up with the wellbeing of biological systems. Their presence impacts the appropriation and conduct of prey species, keeping herbivores from pulverizing vegetation and adjusting the structure of plant networks. This administrative job adds to the general biodiversity and soundness of biological systems.

Biodiversity Preservation:
Tigers are demonstrative of the soundness of their environments. The decay of tiger populaces frequently flags more extensive natural debasement. Monitoring tiger living spaces implies saving the assorted cluster of greenery that coincide in these scenes, encouraging biodiversity and versatility notwithstanding ecological difficulties.

The Case for Worldwide Cooperation: A Common Obligation

Transboundary Nature of Protection:
The protection of tigers intrinsically includes the safeguarding of scenes that length various nations. Tigers don't perceive international limits; their environments stretch out across borders. Successful preservation procedures must, in

this manner, rise above public interests and focus on the common obligation of protecting these transboundary scenes.

Sharing Information and Mastery:

Worldwide cooperation works with the trading of information, mastery, and best practices. Every area confronting tiger protection challenges has novel bits of knowledge and encounters. By sharing this aggregate insight, countries can gain from effective procedures and keep away from traps, speeding up the speed of protection endeavors.

Asset Preparation:

Saving tiger species requires significant monetary assets for against poaching endeavors, living space assurance, and local area commitment. Worldwide co-operation takes into account the pooling of assets, guaranteeing that even mon-etarily tested countries can effectively add to preservation. Worldwide financing components, organizations, and awards become fundamental apparatuses in this joint undertaking.

Political Will and Tact:

The safeguarding of tigers requires solid political will and discretionary endeav-ors. Countries should work together in arranging arrangements, orchestrating strategies, and tending to international difficulties that might ruin preservation drives. Discretionary diverts become vital in encouraging worldwide participa-tion to benefit these brilliant animals.

Examples of overcoming adversity: Instances of Compelling Worldwide Cooperation

The Worldwide Tiger Drive:

Sent off in 2010, the Worldwide Tiger Drive (GTI) remains as a demonstration of the force of worldwide coordinated effort. Driven by the World Bank and including tiger range nations, NGOs, and the global local area, the GTI planned to twofold wild tiger populaces by 2022, the Chinese Year of the Tiger. While the particular objective might not have been accomplished, the drive prodded critical ventures, brought issues to light, and catalyzed a restored obligation to tiger protection universally.

Transboundary Preservation Regions:

A few districts have embraced transboundary preservation models to safeguard tiger territories. The Terai Circular segment Scene, shared by India and Nepal, is a prominent model. The two nations teamed up to lay out the Terai Circular segment Scene program, connecting safeguarded regions across lines to work with the development of tigers and improve hereditary variety.

Worldwide Natural Arrangements:

Peaceful accords and shows, for example, the Show on Worldwide Exchange Jeopardized Types of Wild Fauna and Vegetation (Refers to), give systems to co-operative activity. These arrangements work with correspondence, set principles for natural life insurance, and empower the improvement of composed techniques to battle unlawful untamed life exchange.

Difficulties and Potential open doors for Future Coordinated effort Challenges:

Regardless of the steps made in worldwide cooperation for tiger protection, challenges endure. Public interests, international pressures, and differing levels of responsibility among countries can obstruct coordinated endeavors. Restricted assets, both monetary and human, present boundaries to executing thorough protection procedures. Also, the continuous dangers of environmental change and arising sicknesses further convolute the preservation scene.

Open doors:

As we face these difficulties, there are exceptional open doors for development and coordinated effort. Progresses in innovation, for example, satellite observing, information examination, and computerized reasoning, offer new apparatuses for following tiger populaces and figuring out their way of behaving. The rising acknowledgment of the significance of biodiversity and biological systems administrations in worldwide conversations opens roads for mainstreaming protection objectives into more extensive global plans.

3. **Thesis Statement: Exploring a Comprehensive Approach to Tiger Conservation**

Despite mounting dangers to the endurance of tigers, an extensive way to deal with protection arises as a basic objective. The contemporary difficulties looked by these notable huge felines rise above disconnected protection endeavors and request a comprehensive methodology that envelops natural, financial, and worldwide aspects. This proposal looks to dive into the intricacies of tiger protection, pushing for a multi-layered approach that incorporates logical progressions, local area commitment, and worldwide joint effort.

Figuring out the Direness: Tiger Preservation in the Anthropocene

The Anthropocene time, portrayed by exceptional human impact on the climate, has put tigers near the precarious edge of termination. Quick urbanization, living space misfortune, and the guileful scourge of unlawful untamed life exchange meet to compromise the presence of these glorious animals. The direness of the circumstance requires a takeoff from regular, compartmentalized protection ways to deal with embrace a thorough model that tends to the complicated snare of difficulties looked by tigers in the cutting edge world.

Natural Goal: Adjusting Human Turn of events and Living space Protection

At the center of an extensive methodology lies the acknowledgment that tiger preservation is definitely not a segregated undertaking however a natural goal. Protecting the territories that support these dominant hunters requires a fragile harmony between human turn of events and ecological stewardship. This includes key land-use arranging, the foundation of safeguarded regions, and the making of untamed life passages to relieve the effects of environment discontinuity. By tending to the environmental underpinnings of tiger preservation, we establish the groundwork for supported conjunction among people and these notorious huge felines.

Logical Headways: Utilizing Innovation for Preservation

Headways in innovation offer extraordinary open doors for powerful tiger preservation. From satellite following to DNA investigation, creative apparatuses give important bits of knowledge into tiger conduct, populace elements, and territory well-being. Man-made consciousness and AI calculations further upgrade our capacity to process immense datasets, empowering more exact preservation procedures. This proposal investigates the joining of state of the art advancements into preservation works on, accentuating the job of science in illuminating proof based decision-production for the security of tigers.

Local area Commitment: Engaging Nearby Stewards of Protection

A thorough methodology stretches out past environmental contemplations to incorporate the human component of tiger preservation. Neighborhood people group possessing tiger scenes are not simple spectators but rather vital partners in the safeguarding system. This proposition investigates local area commitment as a foundation of thorough protection, inspecting methodologies that enable nearby occupants as stewards of their normal legacy. Schooling, supportable vocations, and the consideration of native information become vital components in encouraging a feeling of shared liability regarding the prosperity of the two tigers and networks.

The Financial Nexus: Connecting Preservation and Human Government assistance

Tiger preservation can't be separated from the financial settings inside which it works. This postulation investigates the mind boggling nexus among preservation and human government assistance, underlining that the prosperity of networks living in closeness to tiger environments is indivisible from the progress of protection endeavors. Supportable improvement drives, financial other options, and the fair dispersion of protection benefits become fundamental parts of an extensive methodology that recognizes and addresses the financial elements impacting tiger preservation.

Worldwide Coordinated effort: Past Lines for Worldwide Protection Objectives

Perceiving that tigers wander across public limits, an extensive methodology requires global joint effort. This postulation looks at the significance of worldwide organizations in the protection field, underscoring the requirement for shared liability and composed activity. From transboundary preservation drives to discretionary endeavors tending to the main drivers of tiger peril, the investigation of cooperative structures becomes indispensable to the viability of an extensive protection methodology.

Lawful Systems: Fortifying Securities and Discouragement

Lawful systems structure the foundation of powerful preservation. This postulation investigates existing untamed life security regulations, featuring the requirement for their reinforcing and authorization. Discouragement components against poaching and unlawful exchange, combined with worldwide collaboration to destroy criminal organizations, become fundamental in protecting tigers. The investigation of lawful aspects highlights the proposal's obligation to a thorough methodology that tends to both the biological and legitimate features of tiger protection.

Difficulties and Future Possibilities: Exploring the Complicated Scene

As this proposition investigates the thorough way to deal with tiger protection, it basically looks at the difficulties inborn in executing such a complex system. From political contemplations to financial requirements, the perplexing scene of preservation presents jumps that request smart route. The proposal likewise projects a forward-looking look, imagining the possibilities for a future where tigers get by as well as flourish in amicable concurrence with humankind.

In summation, this postulation tries to unwind the layers of a complete way to deal with tiger preservation. By inspecting environmental goals, utilizing logical progressions, drawing in networks, tending to financial elements, cultivating worldwide joint effort, and strengthening legitimate structures, the proposition tries to add to the developing talk on the safeguarding of these notorious huge felines. The earnestness of the ongoing circumstance coaxes us to investigate creative and comprehensive procedures that go past segregated endeavors, fashioning a way toward a future where tigers stay vital parts of our planet's rich embroidery of biodiversity.

Chapter 1

The Global Tiger Landscape

The tiger, a lofty and notable animal groups, has long caught the creative mind of individuals all over the planet. Notwithstanding, the worldwide tiger scene is one set apart by both profound respect for the species' excellence and a profound worry for its endurance. Tigers, once far reaching across Asia, are presently jeopardized, confronting various dangers that have prompted an uncommon decrease in their populaces. This paper will dive into the present status of the worldwide tiger scene, investigating preservation endeavors, the difficulties looked by these wonderful animals, and likely future possibilities for their endurance.

Authentic Setting

By and large, tigers wandered tremendous domains, going from the Siberian taiga to the mangrove marshes of the Sundarbans. Be that as it may, the last century has seen a critical decrease in their living space because of human exercises like deforestation, horticulture, and urbanization. The ascent in human populace and extension of human settlements have prompted expanded struggle among tigers and people, further fueling the difficulties looked by these huge felines.

Protection Endeavors

Perceiving the direness of the circumstance, different preservation drives have been executed universally to safeguard and moderate tiger populaces. One remarkable exertion is the Worldwide Tiger Recuperation Program (GTRP), sent off in 2010 during the St. Petersburg Tiger Highest point. The GTRP means to twofold the quantity of wild tigers by 2022, the following Chinese Year of the Tiger. This drive includes the joint effort of tiger-range nations, worldwide associations, and non-legislative associations (NGOs) to resolve central points of interest like living space misfortune, poaching, and human-tiger clashes.

Public legislatures in tiger-range nations have additionally carried out their own protection programs. India, home to the biggest populace of wild tigers, has the Task Tiger drive, which centers around making untouched spaces for tigers, further developing environment conditions, and including nearby networks in protection endeavors. Comparable drives exist in nations like Russia, Nepal, and Bangladesh, exhibiting a worldwide obligation to protecting these notable animals.

Moreover, the job of non-legislative associations in tiger preservation couldn't possibly be more significant. Associations like the World Untamed life Asset (WWF), the Natural life Preservation Society (WCS), and the Global Association for Preservation of Nature (IUCN) work resolutely to bring issues to light, direct exploration, and asset projects pointed toward safeguarding tigers and their territories.

Challenges Confronting Tigers

Regardless of these preservation endeavors, tigers face a variety of difficulties that compromise their actual presence. One of the main dangers is natural surroundings misfortune. The transformation of woods into agrarian land, logging, and foundation advancement has brought about divided and corrupted natural surroundings for tigers. This diminishes the accessibility of prey as well as increments human-tiger clashes as these wonderful felines are compelled to wander into human-overwhelmed scenes looking for food.

Poaching is another basic issue facing tiger populaces. The interest for tiger parts in conventional Asian medication, combined with the unlawful natural life exchange, represents a serious danger to these creatures. Tigers are frequently focused on for their skins, bones, and other body parts, for certain people succumbing to catches and traps set for different creatures. Regardless of global prohibitions on the exchange of tiger parts, unlawful business sectors endure, driven by popularity and worthwhile benefits.

Human-tiger clashes have heightened as an outcome of contracting environments and waning prey. Tigers, as they continued looking for food, now and again go after animals, prompting retaliatory killings by nearby networks. This pattern of contention further imperils tiger populaces and makes a negative impression of these creatures among nearby occupants.

Environmental change represents an extra test to tiger protection. Climbing temperatures, changing precipitation designs, and the subsequent adjustments in environments can affect both tiger living spaces and their prey. Adjusting to these progressions is critical for the drawn out endurance of tiger populaces.

Mechanical Developments in Preservation

Despite these difficulties, mechanical developments have arisen as integral assets in the preservation tool compartment. Camera traps, for example, have upset untamed life checking. These gadgets catch pictures and recordings of tigers and other untamed life, giving important information to scientists on populace sizes, conduct, and development designs. Moreover, satellite innovation supports planning and observing changes in tiger natural surroundings, assisting traditionalists with settling on informed conclusions about safeguarded regions and passages.

Man-made consciousness (artificial intelligence) and AI are by and large progressively applied to investigate immense measures of information gathered from camera traps and satellite symbolism. These advances empower the distinguishing proof of individual tigers, assisting analysts with following their developments and evaluate populace elements. Computer based intelligence calculations can likewise help with foreseeing and forestalling human-tiger clashes by investigating examples of conduct and distinguishing potential struggle areas of interest.

Drones have become instrumental in looking over immense and testing territories, permitting preservationists to productively screen tiger living spaces more. These automated flying vehicles give a 10,000 foot perspective, supporting the location of criminal operations like poaching and logging. Drones additionally add to against poaching endeavors by watching regions that are challenging to access by walking.

Local area Association and Economical Turn of events

Compelling tiger preservation goes past safeguarding the actual creatures; it includes connecting with nearby networks in maintainable advancement rehearses. Perceiving the significance of local area association, numerous preservation drives currently integrate the requirements and viewpoints of neighborhood occupants.

Local area based preservation projects plan to work out some kind of harmony between human turn of events and untamed life insurance. By including neighborhood networks in dynamic cycles and giving elective livelihoods, these undertakings try to diminish human-natural life clashes and make a common obligation regarding tiger protection. Schooling and mindfulness programs assume a pivotal part in cultivating a deep satisfaction and possession among nearby networks, empowering them to become stewards of their normal legacy.

Manageable The travel industry

Manageable the travel industry addresses one more road for supporting tiger protection. Dependable ecotourism can produce income for nearby networks and add to the financing of preservation programs. Nonetheless, finding some kind of harmony among the travel industry and natural life protection is fundamental. Enthusiastic the travel industry can upset tiger living spaces, disturb their regular way of behaving, and add to pressure among these subtle animals.

Laying out and authorizing rules for moral natural life the travel industry is basic. Appropriate framework, prepared directs, and controlled guest numbers can guarantee that travel industry benefits both neighborhood economies and tiger populaces. Furthermore, income produced from the travel industry can be reinvested in preservation endeavors, making a self-supporting pattern of security and financial turn of events.

Worldwide Coordinated effort

Tigers are not restricted by public boundaries, and their protection requires worldwide cooperation. Tiger range nations should cooperate to address transboundary issues, for example, unlawful untamed life exchange and the network of territories. Associations like the Show on Worldwide Exchange Imperiled Types of Wild Fauna and Verdure (Refers to) assume an imperative part in directing and observing the global exchange tiger parts, working with collaboration among countries to battle poaching and dealing.

Two-sided arrangements and joint drives between nations can fortify protection endeavors. Shared preservation objectives, the trading of skill, and facilitated policing add to the insurance of tigers and their natural surroundings on a worldwide scale. Global financing and backing likewise assume a basic part in guaranteeing the outcome of protection programs in districts where assets might be restricted.

Examples of overcoming adversity and Illustrations Learned

In the midst of the difficulties, there have been examples of overcoming adversity that deal expect the eventual fate of tigers. The case of India, which has seen an expansion in its tiger populace as of late, exhibits the positive effect of centered protection endeavors. The execution of severe enemy of poaching measures, natural surroundings reclamation projects, and local area association has added to the progress of Venture Tiger in India.

Additionally, the renewed introduction of tigers into regions where they had been locally wiped out has demonstrated effective in certain areas. Russia's endeavors to once again introduce Amur tigers in the Far East, for example, have shown promising outcomes. These drives underscore the flexibility of tiger populaces whenever allowed the opportunity to recuperate in reasonable environments with sufficient assurance.

In any case, it is fundamental to perceive that outcome in tiger preservation requires a drawn out responsibility. Preservation endeavors should adjust to evolving conditions, address arising dangers, and constantly draw in with nearby networks. Illustrations gained from effective drives can illuminate future protection systems and move comparable endeavors in different areas confronting difficulties in tiger preservation.

1.1 Distribution of Tiger Habitats Worldwide

The dissemination of tiger territories overall is a basic part of understanding the difficulties and valuable open doors in rationing these famous huge felines. Tigers, having a place with the Panthera tigris species, have generally involved an immense reach across Asia, adjusting to different biological systems. In any case, because of different factors like human infringement, natural surroundings misfortune, and poaching, their conveyance has gone through huge changes.

This paper will investigate the ongoing appropriation of tiger territories around the world, inspecting the key areas where these glorious animals endure and the preservation suggestions related with their geographic reach.

Verifiable Scope of Tigers

By and large, tigers were tracked down across a wide region of Asia, from the Russian Far East to the Indian subcontinent and Southeast Asia. Six subspecies of tigers were perceived in view of their geographic appropriation: Siberian, Bengal, Indochinese, Malayan, South China, and Sumatran tigers. Every subspecies adjusted to explicit conditions, going from the thick backwoods of Siberia to the mangrove bogs of the Sundarbans.

Be that as it may, over the course of the last hundred years, human exercises have essentially modified the scene, prompting a decrease in tiger environments. The extension of agribusiness, logging, and urbanization has divided and lessened the once-far reaching regions these enormous felines meandered.

Current Appropriation of Tiger Environments

1. **Siberian Tigers (Panthera tigris altaica)**

   Siberian tigers, otherwise called Amur tigers, occupy the Russian Far East and portions of northeastern China and North Korea. They are the biggest of all tiger subspecies and are adjusted to the brutal environment of the taiga, a biome portrayed by coniferous backwoods and cold temperatures. Endeavors to ration Siberian tigers incorporate the production of safeguarded regions and drives to address poaching and unlawful logging.

2. **Bengal Tigers (Panthera tigris)**

   Bengal tigers are tracked down principally in India, with more modest populaces in Bangladesh, Bhutan, and Nepal. The Sundarbans, the world's biggest mangrove woods spreading over India and Bangladesh, is a prominent living space for Bengal tigers. India, with its Undertaking Tiger drive, has been at the very front of protection endeavors, laying out stores and hallways to associate divided living spaces.

3. **Indochinese Tigers (Panthera tigris corbetti)**

   Indochinese tigers once ran across Southeast Asia, including Cambodia, Laos, Myanmar, Thailand, and Vietnam. Nonetheless, their populaces have pointedly declined, and they are presently basically jeopardized. Poaching and territory misfortune are significant dangers, and preservation associations are attempting to reinforce hostile to poaching measures and safeguard basic environments.

4. **Malayan Tigers (Panthera tigris jacksoni)**

   Malayan tigers are bound to the Malay Promontory and portions of southern Thailand. The tropical rainforests of this locale give a special territory to these tigers. Deforestation and living space fracture are critical difficulties, stressing the requirement for preservation procedures that address both the assurance of existing environments and the reclamation of debased regions.

5. **South China Tigers (Panthera tigris amoyensis)**

   The South China tiger, one of the most fundamentally imperiled subspecies, was once tracked down in southern China. Be that as it may, it is currently viewed as practically wiped out in the wild, with no realized people getting by. Preservation endeavors center around reproducing programs in imprisonment, with the desire for once again introducing these tigers to their regular natural surroundings later on.

6. Sumatran Tigers (Panthera tigris sumatrae)

Sumatran tigers possess the island of Sumatra in Indonesia. They are adjusted to the island's different biological systems, including marsh backwoods and bumpy districts. Deforestation, unlawful logging, and poaching are significant dangers to Sumatran tigers, and preservation drives expect to safeguard their excess living spaces and address the hidden reasons for their decay.

Protection Difficulties and Systems

1. **Natural surroundings Misfortune and Fracture**
   Natural surroundings misfortune and fracture are among the main difficulties confronting tiger populaces around the world. As human populaces extend and interest for assets increments, normal living spaces are changed over into horticultural land, prompting the fracture of once-coterminous tiger domains. This fracture confines populaces, diminishing hereditary variety and making tigers more powerless against illnesses and ecological changes.
   Preservation methodologies tending to territory misfortune incorporate the production of safeguarded regions, untamed life hallways, and cushion zones. Safeguarded regions, like public stops and holds, give a safe-haven to tigers, while untamed life halls interface divided territories, empowering the development of people between populaces. Support zones, which include working with nearby networks to foster manageable land-use rehearses, expect to diminish human-natural life clashes and advance conjunction.

2. **Human-Natural life Clashes**
   As tiger environments contract, clashes among people and tigers escalate. Tigers might go after domesticated animals, prompting retaliatory killings by nearby networks. Tending to human-natural life clashes requires a multi-layered approach that thinks about the necessities of the two tigers and nearby inhabitants. Local area based preservation drives draw in neighborhood networks in tiger protection, making them partners in the security of these huge felines. By giving elective occupations, carrying out measures to safeguard animals, and including networks in dynamic cycles, traditionalists plan to encourage a feeling of conjunction and shared liability.

3. **Poaching and Unlawful Untamed life Exchange**
   Poaching stays a serious danger to tiger populaces, driven by the interest for tiger parts in customary Asian medication and the unlawful untamed life exchange. Tigers are focused on for their skins, bones, and other body parts, coming down on their populaces.
   To battle poaching, protection associations team up with policing to reinforce hostile to poaching endeavors. This incorporates conveying innovation, for example, camera traps, robots, and satellite observing to follow and prevent

poachers. Also, global collaboration through associations like Refers to is fundamental for address the cross-line nature of the unlawful untamed life exchange.

4. Environmental Change

Environmental change represents an arising danger to tiger natural surroundings. Climbing temperatures, changing precipitation examples, and adjustments in environments can affect both the dispersion of prey species and the accessibility of water sources. Tigers, as dominant hunters, are profoundly reliant upon the wellbeing and soundness of their biological systems.

Adjusting preservation systems to represent environmental change includes making versatile scenes that can endure ecological movements. This might incorporate the reclamation of corrupted natural surroundings, the foundation of environment shrewd passages, and research to comprehend how tigers might answer evolving conditions.

Future Possibilities and Worldwide Cooperation

The eventual fate of tiger living spaces overall relies upon the aggregate endeavors of the worldwide local area. While the difficulties are overwhelming, there are purposes behind hopefulness. Examples of overcoming adversity, like the recuperation of tiger populaces in India and the renewed introduction of tigers in certain locales, show the way that deliberate protection endeavors can yield positive outcomes.

Worldwide joint effort is urgent to address transboundary issues and guarantee the endurance of tigers across their whole reach. Tiger-range nations should share information, assets, and aptitude to execute successful preservation measures.

Global associations, states, NGOs, and nearby networks should cooperate to make a comprehensive methodology that adjusts the necessities of individuals and tigers.

Headways in innovation, for example, man-made reasoning, AI, and robots, give amazing assets to checking and safeguarding tiger living spaces. Proceeded with advancement in these fields can improve our capacity to gather information, break down patterns, and answer arising dangers continuously.

Reasonable advancement that incorporates preservation objectives with the prosperity of neighborhood networks is vital to getting the eventual fate of tiger living spaces. Dependable the travel industry, local area commitment, and the foundation of preservation cordial strategies add to a scene where tigers can flourish close by people.

1.2 Identification of Key Tiger Subspecies

The tiger, Panthera tigris, is an animal varieties that displays wonderful variety across its reach. Inside the overall species, there are a few subspecies, each interestingly adjusted to its particular climate. Distinguishing and understanding these key tiger subspecies is urgent for powerful protection endeavors. This exposition investigates the qualities, appropriation, and preservation status of key tiger subspecies, revealing insight into their unmistakable elements and the difficulties they face in nature.

Authentic Setting and Grouping

All things considered, researchers perceived eight tiger subspecies in view of topographical circulation and particular morphological qualities. Be that as it may, progressions in hereditary examination have prompted a reconsideration of tiger scientific categorization. As of the most recent information, there are currently six perceived subspecies:

Siberian Tiger (Panthera tigris altaica): Otherwise called the Amur tiger, the Siberian tiger is the biggest of all tiger subspecies. It possesses the immense woodlands of the Russian Far East and portions of northeastern China and North Korea.

Bengal Tiger (Panthera tigris): The Bengal tiger is tracked down basically in India, with more modest populaces in Bangladesh, Bhutan, and Nepal. It involves assorted territories, including fields, mangrove swamps, and deciduous backwoods.

Indochinese Tiger (Panthera tigris corbetti): The Indochinese tiger once meandered Southeast Asia, including Cambodia, Laos, Myanmar, Thailand, and Vietnam. Notwithstanding, its populaces have declined fundamentally, and it is presently thought to be basically imperiled.

Malayan Tiger (Panthera tigris jacksoni): Restricted to the Malay Promontory and portions of southern Thailand, the Malayan tiger flourishes in the tropical rainforests of the area.

South China Tiger (Panthera tigris amoyensis): When found in southern China, the South China tiger is viewed as practically terminated in the wild, with people enduring just in imprisonment.

Sumatran Tiger (Panthera tigris sumatrae): Possessing the island of Sumatra in Indonesia, the Sumatran tiger adjusts to different biological systems, including swamp timberlands and rocky areas.

Distinguishing proof of Key Tiger Subspecies

1. **Siberian Tiger (Panthera tigris altaica)**
   Actual Qualities:
   Huge size: Siberian tigers are the biggest among the tiger subspecies, with guys gauging between 400 to 675 pounds and females gauging between 220 to 368 pounds.
   Thick fur: A transformation to the chilly environment, Siberian tigers have a thick, light orange coat with less dull stripes than other subspecies.
   Conveyance:
   Basically saw as in the Russian Far East, including the Sikhote-Alin mountain reach and portions of northeastern China and North Korea.
   Verifiable reach stretched out into Mongolia and conceivably northern China.
   Protection Status:
   Recorded as jeopardized on the Worldwide Association for Protection of Nature (IUCN) Red Rundown.

Preservation endeavors center around safeguarded regions, against poaching measures, and tending to human-tiger clashes.

2. **Bengal Tiger (Panthera tigris)**
Actual Qualities:
Particular coat design: Bengal tigers have a rich orange coat with conspicuous dark stripes that fluctuate in thickness.
White tigers: An uncommon variety tracked down in a Bengal tigers because of a latent quality.
Dissemination:
Mostly tracked down in India, especially in the Sundarbans mangrove woods, meadows, and deciduous woodlands.
More modest populaces in Bangladesh, Bhutan, and Nepal.
Preservation Status:
Delegated jeopardized by the IUCN.
Preservation drives in India incorporate the Venture Tiger program, which lays out tiger holds and spotlights on environment security.

3. **Indochinese Tiger (Panthera tigris corbetti)**
Actual Attributes:
More modest size: Indochinese tigers are for the most part more modest than Bengal and Siberian tigers.
Dim coat: Their jacket is more obscure and their stripes are smaller than those of Bengal tigers.
Appropriation:
Generally went across Southeast Asia, including Cambodia, Laos, Myanmar, Thailand, and Vietnam.
Presently fundamentally jeopardized, with populaces declining because of environment misfortune and poaching.
Preservation Status:
Delegated basically jeopardized by the IUCN.
Preservation endeavors center around safeguarding remaining natural surroundings and reinforcing hostile to poaching measures.

4. **Malayan Tiger (Panthera tigris jacksoni)**
Actual Attributes:
Hazier coat: Malayan tigers have a hazier and more lively orange coat contrasted with other subspecies.
More modest size: They are more modest than Siberian tigers however bigger than Indochinese tigers.
Conveyance:
Bound to the Malay Landmass and portions of southern Thailand.
Occupies the tropical rainforests of the locale.
Preservation Status:

Named fundamentally jeopardized by the IUCN.

Preservation methodologies incorporate territory security, against poaching endeavors, and local area commitment.

5. **South China Tiger (Panthera tigris amoyensis)**

Actual Qualities:

More modest size: South China tigers are more modest than their partners, with a more thin form.

Particular coat: Their jacket has wide, close-set stripes, and they frequently show a lighter hue.

Appropriation:

Generally tracked down in southern China.

As of now thought to be practically terminated in the wild, with people enduring just in bondage.

Protection Status:

Delegated basically jeopardized by the IUCN.

Hostage rearing projects plan to once again introduce the South China tiger to its normal natural surroundings.

6. **Sumatran Tiger (Panthera tigris sumatrae)**

Actual Qualities:

More modest size: Sumatran tigers are the littlest among the tiger subspecies.

Dim coat: Their jacket is more obscure with smaller and closer-set stripes, a transformation to the thick backwoods they possess.

Conveyance:

Occupies the island of Sumatra in Indonesia, including swamp woods and rugged districts.

Preservation Status:

Named fundamentally imperiled by the IUCN.

Preservation endeavors center around safeguarding remaining environments, tending to poaching, and relieving human-natural life clashes.

Preservation Suggestions

Hereditary Variety:

Understanding the hereditary variety of tiger subspecies is critical for their preservation. Escalated inbreeding, frequently saw in disengaged populaces, can prompt hereditary abnormalities and decreased flexibility to evolving conditions. Preservation systems should focus on keeping up with hereditary variety through cautious rearing projects and the formation of halls associating divided environments to work with quality stream.

Environment Jobs:

Every tiger subspecies assumes a special part in its biological system as a dominant hunter. The presence of tigers directs prey populaces, control herbivores, and keep up with the general soundness of biological systems. Accordingly, the decay or eradication of any tiger subspecies can have flowing impacts on the biodiversity and biological equilibrium of their individual territories.

Preservation Needs:

Preservation endeavors should be custom-made to the particular requirements and difficulties looked by every tiger subspecies. For instance, while against poaching measures are basic for all subspecies, systems to address territory misfortune in the thick timberlands of Sumatra might contrast from those expected in the immense taiga of Siberia. Distinguishing and focusing on protection activities in light of the qualities of every subspecies upgrades the adequacy of worldwide tiger preservation drives.

Human-Tiger Clashes:

Understanding the way of behaving and environment of various tiger subspecies is fundamental for alleviating human-tiger clashes. Tigers occupying human-ruled scenes, like the Sundarbans, may require different compromise procedures than those in additional far off regions. Local area commitment and training programs should be customized to the particular setting of every subspecies' natural surroundings to encourage concurrence among people and tigers.

Worldwide Joint effort:

Preserving the variety of tiger subspecies requires global cooperation. Numerous subspecies occupy locales that length various nations, making cross-line collaboration fundamental. Drives like the Worldwide Tiger Recuperation Program and joint effort through global associations like Refers to give structures to nations to cooperate, share assets, and carry out composed preservation methodologies.

1.3 Assessment of Threats to Tiger Populations Globally

The worldwide tiger populace, when flourishing across different environments, faces a bunch of dangers that challenge its presence. Notwithstanding deliberate protection endeavors, tiger populaces have been waning, and a few subspecies are presently fundamentally imperiled. This paper gives a complete evaluation of the dangers facing tiger populaces around the world, digging into the diverse difficulties adding to their downfall and investigating likely systems for relieving these dangers.

1. **Living space Misfortune and Discontinuity:**

   Living space misfortune arises as a principal danger to worldwide tiger populaces. The extending human impression, driven by agribusiness, foundation improvement, and urbanization, has brought about the debasement and discontinuity of basic tiger natural surroundings. The results are significant.

   The effect of living space misfortune is twofold. Right off the bat, tigers, being regional dominant hunters, require broad domains for hunting, reproducing, and keeping up with their predominance. The decrease in reasonable territories limits these great felines to more modest spaces, improving the probability of human-untamed life clashes. Tigers frequently adventure into human-ruled scenes, putting them in conflict with nearby networks.

Also, environment discontinuity separates tiger populaces. This confinement not just hinders the regular development and dispersal of people yet in addition lessens hereditary variety. Diminished hereditary variety makes tiger populaces more helpless against illnesses and less versatile to natural changes, imperiling their drawn out feasibility.

Moderating environment misfortune includes diverse procedures. Laying out and keeping up with safeguarded regions, like public stops and saves, are critical stages in protecting flawless tiger environments. Moreover, making natural life hallways that associate divided regions permits tigers to move uninhibitedly between separated populaces, cultivating hereditary variety and advancing the soundness of biological systems. Local area commitment assumes a pivotal part by including nearby networks in feasible land-use works on, making cradle zones around safeguarded regions, and tending to the main drivers of natural surroundings misfortune.

2. **Poaching and Unlawful Untamed life Exchange:**
Poaching stays a constant and serious danger to tiger populaces worldwide, driven by the interest for tiger parts in customary Asian medication and the unlawful untamed life exchange. Regardless of global endeavors to check such exercises, the effect on tiger populaces keeps on being disturbing.

The effect of poaching stretches out past quick populace decrease. Tigers are dominant hunters with huge jobs in keeping up with environmental equilibrium. Tenacious poaching upsets their normal ways of behaving, possibly prompting lopsided characteristics in prey populaces and flowing impacts all through environments.

The unlawful natural life exchange intensifies the danger presented by poaching. In spite of global restrictions on the exchange of tiger parts, the interest for these items continues. This propagates a pattern of double-dealing that further jeopardizes tiger populaces.

Tending to poaching requires a diverse methodology. Reinforcing on-the-ground hostile to poaching measures, utilizing innovation, for example, camera traps and robots for observing and watching, and working on global joint effort through associations like Refers to are fundamental parts of the arrangement. Furthermore, public mindfulness crusades assume a critical part in diminishing the interest for tiger items, cultivating a feeling of obligation and compassion toward these imperiled species.

3. **Human-Untamed life Clashes:**
The contracting of tiger territories strengthens clashes among people and tigers, introducing one more huge danger to worldwide tiger populaces. As tigers adventure into human-overwhelmed scenes looking for food, they frequently come into contact with nearby networks, prompting clashes that have sweeping

results.

The effect of human-natural life clashes is two-sided. On one hand, tigers might go after domesticated animals, inciting retaliatory killings by neighborhood networks trying to safeguard their occupations. These retaliatory killings diminish tiger populaces as well as add to negative view of these magnificent creatures among neighborhood occupants.

Moderating human-natural life clashes requires a nuanced and local area centered approach. Including neighborhood networks in dynamic cycles and making mindfulness about the significance of conjunction can assist with cultivating a feeling of shared liability regarding tiger preservation. Carrying out elective business programs and manageable land-use practices can additionally diminish the financial tensions driving struggles. Eventually, making an agreeable harmony between human necessities and tiger preservation is fundamental for the drawn out conjunction of both.

4. **Environmental Change:**

Environmental change has arisen as an undeniably huge danger to tiger populaces all around the world. The adjustments in temperature, precipitation examples, and generally biological system elements influence both tiger territories and their prey species.

The effect of environmental change is complex. Changes in temperature and precipitation can straightforwardly influence the accessibility of water sources, affecting the conveyance of prey species and adjusting the general scene.

These changes, thus, challenge the versatility of tigers and their capacity to flourish in their customary natural surroundings.

Adjusting protection systems to represent environmental change includes a few key contemplations. Reclamation of debased territories and the foundation of environment savvy hallways that work with the development of species in light of changing circumstances are urgent. Furthermore, examination into how tigers might answer ecological movements is fundamental for creating proactive and versatile protection measures.

Chapter 2

Historical Perspectives On Tiger Conservation

Tigers, sublime and cryptic dominant hunters, have enraptured human creative mind for a really long time. Notwithstanding, the historical backdrop of our relationship with these huge felines has been set apart by both reverence and struggle. As human social orders have advanced, so too affects tiger populaces. This exposition dives into the verifiable points of view on tiger protection, following the intricate interchange among people and tigers after some time. From old social imagery to the cutting edge difficulties of preservation, understanding this verifiable setting is significant for concocting successful procedures to guarantee the endurance of these notorious species.

Tigers in Old Societies

Imagery and Folklore:

Tigers have held representative importance in different antiquated societies, frequently addressing power, strength, and profound importance. In Hindu folklore, the goddess Durga is portrayed riding a tiger, representing her heavenly strength. Additionally, Chinese folklore connects the tiger with mental fortitude and insurance against fiendish spirits.

These social portrayals added to a specific veneration for tigers, molding the manner in which networks apparent and cooperated with these magnificent animals. Tigers were appreciated for their actual ability as well as implanted in the profound and social texture of social orders.

Illustrious Hunting:

Rather than their emblematic significance, tigers confronted critical dangers because of human exercises, especially illustrious hunting rehearses. In old times, rulers and blue-bloods participated in intricate tiger chases as presentations of force and ability. Tigers were pursued for their skins, bones, and other body parts, adding to the decay of neighborhood populaces.

While tiger hunting had social and authentic importance, it additionally laid the basis for the abuse and risk of tiger populaces. As social orders progressed from conventional to additional industrialized structures, the effect on tiger living spaces and populaces turned out to be more articulated.

Frontier Period and Abuse

English Pilgrim Impact:

The pilgrim time additionally increased the abuse of tiger populaces. English pilgrim rulers, especially in India, took part in enormous scope chasing after sport. Tigers were seen as a danger to domesticated animals and human settlements, prompting broad separating endeavors. The presentation of guns exacerbated the hunting tension on tigers, driving a few populaces to the edge of eradication.

The frontier heritage left an enduring effect on tiger living spaces and populaces. Deforestation, driven by the interest for wood and farming extension, further reduced reasonable environments for these enormous felines. The double-dealing of regular assets and natural life during the pioneer time frame set up for the difficulties looked by tiger preservation in the advanced period.

Early Protection Endeavors

Change in Perspectives:

The late nineteenth and mid twentieth hundreds of years saw a steady change in perspectives towards untamed life, driven to some degree by crafted by early progressives. Compelling figures, for example, Jim Corbett in India and Peter Matthiessen in the US started supporting for the security of tigers and their living spaces. Their compositions and promotion assumed a significant part in bringing issues to light about the requirement for protection.

The foundation of public parks and natural life safe-havens, like Yellowstone Public Park in the US and Jim Corbett Public Park in India, denoted a critical takeoff from prior perspectives of double-dealing. These safeguarded regions gave shelters to natural life, including tigers, and set up for more extensive protection endeavors.

Present day Protection Difficulties

Territory Misfortune and Fracture:

The last 50% of the twentieth hundred years and the mid 21st century brought new difficulties for tiger protection. Fast human populace development, urbanization, and farming extension prompted broad territory misfortune and fracture. Tigers, adjusted to enormous and ceaseless scenes, wound up bound to disengaged pockets, making them more powerless against different dangers.

Poaching and Unlawful Natural life Exchange:

Poaching for the unlawful natural life exchange arose as difficult for tiger protection. Interest for tiger bones, skins, and other body parts endured, driven by customary medication rehearses and a rewarding underground market. Notwithstanding worldwide endeavors to check the unlawful untamed life exchange, poaching stayed an imposing danger to tiger populaces, especially in locales where requirement was powerless.

Human-Natural life Clashes:

As human populaces kept on infringing upon tiger environments, clashes among people and tigers raised. Tigers going after animals prompted retaliatory killings by neighborhood networks, making a pattern of contention that compromised both human and tiger populaces. Adjusting the necessities of nearby networks with the preservation goals for tigers turned into a mind boggling challenge.

Worldwide Preservation Drives

Worldwide Tiger Recuperation Program:

Perceiving the requirement for composed endeavors, worldwide drives, for example, the Worldwide Tiger Recuperation Program (GTRP) were sent off. The GTRP, started in 2010, expected to twofold the worldwide tiger populace by 2022 and zeroed in on safeguarding tiger living spaces, upgrading hostile to poaching endeavors, and drawing in with neighborhood networks. The GTRP featured the significance of cooperation among tiger-range nations and worldwide associations for the progress of protection attempts.

St. Petersburg Tiger Highest point:

The St. Petersburg Tiger Highest point in 2010 united world pioneers to examine and focus on tiger preservation. The culmination brought about the Worldwide Tiger Drive, which underscored an all encompassing way to deal with tiger preservation, incorporating environment security, hostile to poaching measures, and local area commitment.

Protection Advances:

Headways in innovation play had an essential impact in current tiger preservation. Camera traps, satellite following, and Geographic Data Framework (GIS) innovation have reformed the observing and examination of tiger populaces. These apparatuses give significant information to progressives, empowering them to follow tiger developments, evaluate populace wellbeing, and answer arising dangers continuously.

Contemporary Protection Techniques

Safeguarded Regions and Hall Network:

Saving and extending safeguarded regions stays a foundation of tiger protection. Making and keeping up with halls that interface divided territories permit tigers to move uninhibitedly, advancing quality stream and keeping up with hereditary variety. These actions assist with tending to the difficulties presented by living space misfortune and fracture.

Against Poaching Measures and Policing:

Reinforcing against poaching measures is basic for battling the unlawful untamed life exchange. Sending thoroughly prepared and prepared enemy of poaching units, using innovation, for example, robots and camera traps, and further developing policing are fundamental parts of powerful preservation techniques. Joint effort with neighborhood networks to deter poaching and bring issues to light about the significance of tiger preservation is similarly essential.

Local area Commitment and Occupation Drives:

Connecting with nearby networks in preservation endeavors is crucial for the outcome of tiger protection. Local area based drives that give elective vocations, include neighborhood occupants in dynamic cycles, and address the underlying drivers of human-untamed life clashes cultivate a feeling of shared liability and advance concurrence.

Economical Turn of events and Environment Flexibility:

Coordinating tiger protection with manageable improvement objectives is basic for long haul achievement. Mindful the travel industry, supportable land-use practices, and strategies that offset monetary improvement with natural protection add to a scene where tigers can flourish close by human networks. Additionally, considering in environment strength in protection procedures guarantees that tiger territories can adjust to changing ecological circumstances.

2.1 Evolution of Conservation Efforts Over the Years

The development of preservation endeavors throughout the years mirrors a unique excursion set apart by having an impact on points of view, developing mindfulness, and a rising need to get a move on to safeguard the planet's biodiversity. From the early acknowledgment of the need to protect regular assets to the foundation of current preservation structures, this article investigates the key achievements, approaches, and difficulties in the advancement of protection endeavors.

Early Preservation Ideas

Native Practices:

Well before the formalization of preservation as a discipline, native networks all over the planet rehearsed feasible asset the executives. Native information frameworks underlined an agreeable relationship with nature, perceiving the interconnectedness of environments. Practices like rotational horticulture, controlled consumes, and feasible hunting showed a comprehension of the need to keep up with natural equilibrium.

Starting points of Untamed life Insurance:

In the nineteenth hundred years, worries about the effect of human exercises on untamed life started to arise. In light of overhunting and living space annihilation, early progressives supported for the security of specific species. The foundation of Yellowstone Public Park in the US in 1872 is in many cases considered the main huge move toward formalizing the security of normal scenes and untamed life.

The Preservation Development

Ascent of Preservation Associations:

The late nineteenth and mid twentieth hundreds of years saw the rise of preservation associations committed to the security of nature. The Boone and Crockett Club, established in 1887, assumed a vital part in supporting for natural life preservation in North America. The foundation of the Sierra Club in 1892 denoted another achievement, zeroing in on saving wild regions and advancing ecological stewardship.

Theodore Roosevelt and Preservation Strategy:

Theodore Roosevelt, the 26th Leader of the US, is many times hailed as a progressive chief. His administration (1901-1909) saw the formation of the US Woodland Administration, the foundation of five public parks, and the marking of the Artifacts Act, permitting the president to assign public landmarks. Roosevelt's protection arrangements established the groundwork for the more extensive preservation development.

Aldo Leopold and the Land Ethic:

Aldo Leopold, a famous scientist and creator, contributed essentially to the moral underpinnings of protection. His paper "The Land Ethic," distributed in his book "A Sand Province Chronicle" in 1949, contended for an extended moral system that incorporates the land as a local area to be regarded and safeguarded. Leopold's thoughts affected the advancement of natural morals and preservation reasoning.

Worldwide Protection Endeavors

Foundation of Public Parks:

The idea of public parks built up some momentum in the mid twentieth hundred years. Nations all over the planet started assigning regions as public parks to safeguard regular and social legacy. Banff Public Park in Canada, laid out in 1885, is quite possibly of the earliest model. Saving assigned regions for their characteristic worth turned into a foundation of preservation endeavors.

Transitory Bird Deal Act:

The Transitory Bird Deal Demonstration of 1918 denoted a pivotal move toward global collaboration for untamed life protection. The arrangement between the US and Canada intended to safeguard transient birds by controlling hunting and guaranteeing environment conservation. Ensuing deals extended the extent of worldwide coordinated effort in defending transient species.

Worldwide Association for Preservation of Nature (IUCN):

Laid out in 1948, the IUCN turned into a worldwide power for preservation. Uniting legislatures, NGOs, and researchers, the IUCN assumed a key part in creating protection systems, surveying the preservation status of species, and cultivating worldwide collaboration. The IUCN Red Rundown, first distributed in 1964, turned into a fundamental device for observing the situation with undermined species around the world.

Present day Preservation Approaches

Protection Science as a Discipline:

The late twentieth century saw the development of preservation science as a particular logical discipline. Protection scholars applied natural standards, hereditary qualities, and other logical apparatuses to comprehend and address the difficulties looked by jeopardized species and biological systems. This interdisciplinary methodology carried meticulousness and accuracy to protection rehearses.

Reasonable Turn of events and Biodiversity Protection:

The idea of reasonable improvement acquired unmistakable quality in the late twentieth hundred years as a reaction to the acknowledgment that preservation ought not be separated from more extensive financial contemplations. The Brundtland Commission's meaning of practical advancement in 1987 accentuated addressing the requirements of the present without compromising the capacity of people in the future to address their own issues. This all encompassing methodology coordinated ecological, social, and monetary contemplations into preservation arranging.

Show on Natural Variety (CBD):

The Unified Countries Show on Natural Variety, endorsed at the Earth Culmination in 1992, denoted a milestone understanding among countries to preserve biodiversity, use assets reasonably, and guarantee the fair and impartial sharing of advantages. The CBD turned into a structure for global participation on biodiversity protection, determined to accomplish a fair and maintainable connection among people and the normal world.

Scene and Environment Based Preservation:

Preservation endeavors progressively moved towards scene and environment based approaches. Perceiving the interconnectedness of species and natural surroundings, moderates underlined the significance of protecting whole environments. This approach thought about safeguarded regions as well as the encompassing scenes and halls basic for keeping up with environmental cycles.

Difficulties and Contemporary Preservation Issues

Environmental Change and Preservation:

The 21st century carried another arrangement of difficulties to preservation endeavors, with environmental change arising as a basic variable. Climbing temperatures, changing precipitation examples, and outrageous climate occasions present critical dangers to biological systems and species. Preservation techniques currently consolidate environment versatility and transformation measures to address the effects of a quickly evolving environment.

Human-Untamed life Struggle:

As human populaces proceed to develop and infringe upon normal territories, clashes among people and untamed life have raised. Rivalry for assets, territory discontinuity, and retaliatory killings present dangers to both untamed life and human networks. Protection systems currently incorporate compromise measures and local area commitment to address these difficulties.

Mechanical Advancements in Preservation:

Headways in innovation have changed preservation rehearses. Remote detecting, satellite symbolism, camera traps, and DNA examination have become fundamental devices for observing and concentrating on natural life. These innovations improve how we might interpret biological systems as well as add to more compelling preservation procedures and versatile administration.

Preservation Money and Confidential Area Commitment:

Getting financing for protection projects has forever been a test. As of late, there has been a developing acknowledgment of the requirement for inventive supporting components. Public-private associations, eco-the travel industry drives, and biodiversity offset programs include the confidential area in preservation endeavors while offering monetary help for protection projects.

2.2 Lessons Learned from Previous Challenges

Preservation endeavors, crossing hundreds of years, have explored through a mind boggling scene of difficulties and wins. Pondering previous encounters gives significant experiences into the complexities of shielding biodiversity. This paper dives into key examples gained from past difficulties in preservation, offering a guide for exploring the current and future intricacies in the undertaking to safeguard our planet's biological systems.

1. **Perceiving Interconnectedness:**
   One significant example from past difficulties is the acknowledgment of the interconnectedness of species and biological systems. Early preservation endeavors frequently centered around individual species or leader creatures without completely getting a handle on the many-sided trap of natural connections. As we noticed the outcomes of such thin methodologies, contemporary preservation has moved towards comprehensive systems that focus on whole environments.

   Grasping the fragile harmony between species, natural surroundings, and ecological cycles is critical. Preservation drives currently perceive that safeguarding a solitary animal categories requires saving its territory, guaranteeing the endurance of prey species, and keeping up with the biological administrations given by the whole environment. This interconnected viewpoint has informed scene and environment based approaches, stressing the need to shield biodiversity on a more extensive scale.

2. **Integrating Native Information:**
   Native people group, with their profound association with nature, have shown manageable practices for ages. Early preservation endeavors frequently ignored or excused native information. In any case, the examples gained from these networks highlight the significance of integrating customary thinking into contemporary preservation techniques.

   Native practices, like rotational farming, controlled consumes, and local area based asset the board, offer important experiences into keeping up with biological equilibrium. Perceiving and regarding native viewpoints adds to compelling protection as well as cultivates organizations based on common comprehension and shared stewardship of the climate.

3. **Adjusting Safeguarding and Usage:**
   By and large, protection drives confronted difficulties in tracking down the right

harmony among safeguarding and usage of regular assets. The 'fort preservation' model, which zeroed in on rigorously safeguarding regions disregarding the requirements of nearby networks, frequently prompted clashes and restricted achievement.

A basic example learned is the significance of coordinating preservation with practical turn of events. Perceiving the requirements of nearby networks for assets and occupations, while guaranteeing capable asset the board, makes a mutually beneficial situation. Protection endeavors that consolidate the standards of manageable improvement are bound to acquire neighborhood support, encouraging a feeling of shared liability regarding the climate.

4. **Adjusting to Evolving Conditions:**

   The effects of environmental change present a huge contemporary test, yet the examples from adjusting to changing conditions have profound verifiable roots. Protection endeavors have figured out how to be versatile and receptive to moving climatic circumstances.

   Early preservation drives frequently expected a static climate, however the present methodologies recognize the powerful idea of biological systems. Building strength in protection arranging includes understanding how species and natural surroundings can adjust to changing climatic circumstances. This incorporates the distinguishing proof and security of environment versatile territories, as well as making halls that work with the development of species in light of natural changes.

5. **Connecting with Neighborhood People group:**

   One of the most basic examples learned is the essential job of nearby networks in preservation. By and large, protection endeavors now and again dismissed or minimized the necessities and viewpoints of those living in closeness to natural life environments. The outcomes were much of the time uplifted human-untamed life clashes and protection from preservation measures.

   Successful preservation currently puts areas of strength for an on local area commitment. Perceiving the privileges and interests of neighborhood networks, including them in dynamic cycles, and guaranteeing that protection drives benefit them straightforwardly add to the achievement and manageability of tasks. Networks are partners as well as fundamental accomplices in the protection venture.

6. **Utilizing Innovation for Protection:**

   Headways in innovation have changed protection works on, offering useful assets for exploration, observing, and versatile administration. Examples from past difficulties feature the significance of embracing mechanical developments to upgrade the adequacy of preservation endeavors.

   Innovative apparatuses, for example, satellite symbolism, remote detecting, camera traps, and hereditary examination have become basic to protection science.

These devices give constant information, empower effective observing of species and environments, and add to confirm based direction.

The capacity to adjust and use arising advancements outfits preservationists with the devices important to address complex difficulties.

7. **Advancing Training and Mindfulness:**

Early preservation endeavors frequently battled with restricted public mindfulness and comprehension of the significance of biodiversity. The acknowledgment that protection achievement relies upon public help has prompted a more grounded accentuation on instruction and mindfulness.

Example learned is that powerful preservation requires logical mastery as well as a more extensive cultural responsibility. Connecting with general society through instructive projects, mindfulness missions, and resident science drives encourages a feeling of obligation and proprietorship. Educated and persuaded networks are bound to help preservation strategies, advocate for security gauges, and add to long haul maintainability.

8. **Embracing Versatile Administration:**

The eccentric idea of natural frameworks requires a versatile administration approach. Progressives have discovered that techniques should be adaptable and receptive to developing circumstances, vulnerabilities, and unexpected difficulties.

Executing versatile administration includes persistent checking and assessment of preservation drives. On the off chance that a specific methodology demonstrates ineffectual or on the other hand assuming that new dangers arise, the system can be changed likewise. This iterative cycle recognizes that protection is a continuous, unique exertion that requires steady learning and variation.

9. **Advancing Worldwide Coordinated effort:**

Preservation challenges frequently rise above political limits, and effective protection requires worldwide joint effort. Early endeavors were in some cases obliged by international contemplations and coming up short on worldwide viewpoint. The present preservation drives benefit from illustrations found out about the significance of joint effort at the worldwide level.

Worldwide issues, for example, environmental change, natural life dealing, and territory misfortune request composed endeavors. Worldwide associations, arrangements, and cooperative stages unite different partners to share information, assets, and obligations. Examples from past difficulties highlight the need of worldwide collaboration for successful protection results.

Chapter 3

International Organizations And Collaborations

Chasing worldwide protection objectives, the job of global associations and coordinated efforts couldn't possibly be more significant. The intricacy of natural difficulties, going from biodiversity misfortune and environment corruption to environmental change and unlawful untamed life exchange, requires a unified, cross-line approach. This far reaching examination investigates the scene of worldwide associations associated with preservation, the cooperative structures they work inside, and the effect of their aggregate endeavors on worldwide biodiversity.

1. **The Scene of Global Protection Associations**
1. **Joined Countries Climate Program (UNEP)**
   The Unified Countries Climate Program, laid out in 1972, is a key worldwide association zeroing in on natural issues, including preservation. UNEP works with cooperation among countries, arranges ecological exercises, and supports the improvement of global natural regulation. Inside its degree, UNEP tends to biodiversity protection through different projects and drives.
2. **Show on Organic Variety (CBD)**
   The Show on Organic Variety, took on during the Earth Culmination in 1992, is a significant global settlement that perceives the significance of rationing biodiversity and advancing maintainable use. CBD gives a structure to nations to foster public biodiversity systems, set targets, and team up on issues like natural surroundings insurance, feasible asset the board, and the fair sharing of advantages emerging from biodiversity.
3. **Worldwide Association for Protection of Nature (IUCN)**
   The Worldwide Association for Protection of Nature, established in 1948, is a worldwide expert on the situation with the regular world. IUCN works as an organization of part associations, legislatures, and specialists, pursuing educated and viable protection activities. The IUCN Red Rundown of Undermined

Species, an extensive data set evaluating the eradication chance of species, is a prominent commitment to worldwide preservation endeavors.

4. **World Untamed life Asset (WWF)**

   The World Natural life Asset, laid out in 1961, is a non-legislative association with a worldwide presence. WWF teams up with state run administrations, organizations, and networks to address ecological difficulties, including environment safeguarding, environmental change, and maintainable turn of events. WWF assumes a pivotal part in forming protection strategies and executing on-the-ground drives.

5. **Natural life Protection Society (WCS)**

   The Natural life Protection Society, established in 1895, works as a worldwide association devoted to saving natural life and wild places. With an emphasis on science, WCS conducts hands on work, oversees preservation programs, and draws in with nearby networks. The association's exercises length a great many biological systems, adding to the insurance of jeopardized species and their territories.

6. **Bonn Show (CMS)**

   The Show on the Protection of Transitory Types of Wild Creatures, otherwise called the Bonn Show or CMS, plans to moderate earthbound, sea-going, and avian transient species. CMS works under the Assembled Countries Climate Program and works with global participation for the protection of species that cross public limits.

7. **Ramsar Show on Wetlands**

The Ramsar Show, laid out in 1971, centers around the preservation and supportable utilization of wetlands. Wetlands assume an essential part in supporting biodiversity, and the Ramsar Show gives a structure to global joint effort in the security of these crucial environments.

II. Cooperative Systems for Preservation

1. **Worldwide Ecological Office (GEF)**

   The Worldwide Climate Office fills in as a monetary component for a few global ecological shows, including the CBD. GEF gives subsidizing to help projects tending to biodiversity protection, environmental change, land corruption, and that's only the tip of the iceberg. By preparing assets and advancing coordinated effort, GEF assumes a focal part in executing worldwide natural arrangements.

2. **Joined Countries Advancement Program (UNDP)**

   The Unified Countries Improvement Program deals with an expansive range of worldwide difficulties, including natural maintainability and protection. UNDP teams up with nations to incorporate ecological contemplations into improvement arranging, underscoring the interconnectedness of protection and human prosperity.

3. **Joined Countries Structure Show on Environmental Change (UNFCCC)**
While basically centered around environmental change, the UNFCCC perceives the necessary association among environment and biodiversity. Drives like Decreasing Discharges from Deforestation and Woods Corruption (REDD+) under UNFCCC add to both environment relief and biodiversity preservation by tending to deforestation and advancing reasonable land use.

4. **Intergovernmental Science-Strategy Stage on Biodiversity and Environment Administrations (IPBES)**
Laid out in 2012, IPBES capabilities as an intergovernmental body that evaluates the condition of biodiversity, biological systems, and the administrations they give to society. By overcoming any issues among science and strategy, IPBES adds to educated independent direction and the advancement regarding compelling protection techniques.

5. **Alliance of the Willing on Pollinators**

Perceiving the crucial job of pollinators in keeping up with biodiversity and worldwide food security, the Alliance of the Willing on Pollinators arose as a cooperative exertion. This alliance plans to address the decay of pollinators by advancing feasible farming, living space protection, and the decrease of pesticide use.

III. Examples of overcoming adversity and Difficulties in Worldwide Protection Coordinated efforts

1. **Examples of overcoming adversity**
Panda Preservation in China (WWF): Cooperative endeavors between the Chinese government and WWF have prompted critical accomplishments in panda protection. Through environment insurance, local area commitment, and hostile to poaching measures, the monster panda populace has seen a positive direction.
African Elephant Protection (Refers to): The Show on Global Exchange Imperiled Types of Wild Fauna and Greenery (Refers to) plays had a significant impact in directing the worldwide exchange of African elephants and their ivory. The coordinated effort among part nations has added to a decrease in unlawful ivory exchange.
Coral Reef Security (Global Coral Reef Drive): The Worldwide Coral Reef Drive (ICRI) unites state run administrations, NGOs, and worldwide associations to address the dangers confronting coral reefs. Through facilitated activity, ICRI has added to the foundation of marine safeguarded regions and feasible fisheries the executives.

2. **Challenges and Annoying Issues**

Unlawful Natural life Exchange: In spite of worldwide endeavors, unlawful untamed life exchange stays a huge test. Poaching and dealing of imperiled species continue because of interest for fascinating pets, customary drugs, and extravagance products. Upgraded cooperation and stricter implementation are expected to battle this unlawful exchange.

Environmental Change Effects: The cooperative structures tending to environmental change and biodiversity frequently work autonomously. Environmental change represents an extreme danger to biodiversity, and incorporating preservation endeavors with environment relief and variation systems stays a perplexing test.

Restricted Subsidizing and Asset Portion: Numerous protection drives face requirements because of restricted financing and assets. While associations like GEF assume an essential part, tending to the size of biodiversity misfortune requires expanded monetary responsibilities from the worldwide local area.

V. Arising Patterns and Future Headings

1. **Innovation and Advancement**

   Headways in innovation, like satellite observing, man-made brainpower, and DNA examination, are changing protection endeavors. These apparatuses upgrade information assortment, observing, and implementation, giving more viable means to address dangers like environment misfortune and unlawful natural life exchange.

2. **Nature-Based Arrangements**

   Nature-based arrangements include outfitting the force of biological systems to address ecological difficulties. This approach accentuates the rebuilding and feasible administration of environments to accomplish biodiversity preservation, environment flexibility, and human prosperity.

3. **Comprehensive Protection**

   Perceiving the significance of inclusivity, protection drives are progressively including nearby networks, native people groups, and underestimated gatherings. Comprehensive protection not just regards the privileges and information on these networks yet additionally fortifies the supportability and progress of preservation projects.

4. **Strategy Coordination**

   Endeavors are in progress to coordinate biodiversity contemplations into more extensive arrangement systems. By adjusting protection objectives to economical turn of events, environment, and land-use strategies, a more sound and synergistic way to deal with tending to interconnected difficulties is arising.

5. **Worldwide Pandemics and Protection**

The Coronavirus pandemic has featured the interconnectedness of human and ecological wellbeing. Protection endeavors are progressively recognizing the connection between living space debasement, untamed life exchange, and the gamble of zoonotic illnesses, stressing the requirement for a One Wellbeing approach that thinks about the soundness of environments, natural life, and people together.

V. Determination: Towards a Feasible Future

Worldwide associations and coordinated efforts assume a crucial part in molding the direction of worldwide protection endeavors. The examples gained from past victories and difficulties give an establishment to building more powerful, comprehensive, and creative systems. As we explore the intricacies of the 21st hundred years, the cooperative soul exemplified by these associations stays fundamental for making an economical future where biodiversity flourishes, biological systems prosper, and humankind coincides agreeably with the normal world.

3.1 Role of Wildlife Conservation Groups

Untamed life preservation gatherings, frequently working as non-administrative associations (NGOs), have become instrumental players in the worldwide work to secure and protect the world's biodiversity. These associations commit their endeavors to tending to the horde challenges looked by untamed life, going from territory misfortune and unlawful natural life exchange to environmental change and human-untamed life clashes. This paper investigates the complex job of untamed life protection gatherings, digging into their capabilities, influence, and the provokes they explore in their main goal to defend Earth's assorted environments.

1. **Environment Insurance and Reclamation**

   Untamed life preservation bunches effectively take part in the security and reclamation of regular environments, remembering them as the groundwork of biodiversity. By obtaining and overseeing land for protection purposes, these associations make safe-havens and stores that act as shelters for different species. The Nature Conservancy, for instance, is prestigious for its work in getting biologically huge terrains across the globe, utilizing methodologies that balance the necessities of both untamed life and nearby networks.

   In addition, these gatherings frequently embrace environment reclamation drives, planning to restore biological systems that have been debased by human exercises. Rebuilding activities might include establishing local vegetation, once again introducing cornerstone species, and carrying out economical land the executives rehearses. By zeroing in on living space assurance and rebuilding, preservation bunches add to the general strength of environments and the endurance of incalculable species.

2. **Species Preservation and Jeopardized Species Recuperation**

   A focal point of natural life protection bunches is the preservation of individual species, especially those confronting inescapable dangers or elimination. The World Natural life Asset (WWF), for example, has been at the very front of species protection endeavors around the world. These gatherings direct examination to survey the situation with species, distinguish key dangers, and foster designated protection plans.

Imperiled species recuperation programs, frequently started and carried out by these gatherings, include a blend of hostage rearing, natural surroundings security, and local area commitment. The endeavors to save the California condor, drove by associations like the Ventana Natural life Society, epitomize the commitment expected for the recuperation of fundamentally jeopardized species. By working cooperatively with legislative organizations, neighborhood networks, and different partners, natural life preservation bunches assume an essential part in forestalling the termination of weak species.

3. **Against Poaching and Natural life Policing**

   Poaching, driven by the unlawful untamed life exchange, stays a huge danger to various species, including elephants, rhinos, and large felines. Untamed life preservation bunches effectively take part in enemy of poaching endeavors, conveying groups on the ground to safeguard designated species. The Worldwide Enemy of Poaching Establishment (IAPF) is an illustration of an association that spotlights on preparing and sending hostile to poaching units in locales with elevated degrees of poaching movement.

   These gatherings frequently team up with nearby policing, offering help, assets, and ability to improve natural life policing. Moreover, they advocate for more grounded lawful systems and punishments to stop poaching exercises. Through these drives, natural life protection bunches add to the assurance of notable species and the safeguarding of biodiversity.

4. **Local area Commitment and Supportable Turn of events**

   Perceiving the significance of neighborhood networks in protection endeavors, natural life preservation bunches progressively stress local area commitment and practical turn of events. The Untamed life Protection Society (WCS), for example, coordinates preservation with local area based drives in a considerable lot of its undertakings. These drives expect to engage nearby networks, give elective occupations, and advance maintainable asset the board rehearses.

   By including networks in the dynamic cycles and guaranteeing that preservation endeavors line up with their requirements, these gatherings fabricate organizations that are fundamental for long haul achievement. The making of local area drove preservation regions and the foundation of conservancies, where neighborhood networks effectively take part in natural life protection, are instances of the positive results of such cooperative methodologies.

5. **Support and Strategy Impact**

   Natural life preservation bunches assume a vital part in support, impacting strategies at nearby, public, and worldwide levels. Through research, campaigning, and public mindfulness crusades, these associations endeavor to shape arrangements that focus on biodiversity preservation. The Rainforest Establishment, for example, advocates for arrangements that battle deforestation and safeguard the privileges of native networks whose jobs are intently attached to the timberland.

These gatherings additionally draw in with administrative bodies, partaking in discussions and talks to guarantee that protection contemplations are implanted in authoritative structures. By impacting strategy, untamed life protection bunches add to the making of an empowering climate for compelling preservation measures.

6. **Research and Logical Advancement**

The quest for powerful preservation systems depends vigorously on logical information and examination. Natural life protection bunches are effectively associated with logical undertakings, leading investigations on species conduct, populace elements, and the effect of ecological changes. Associations, for example, the Middle for Natural Variety center around logical examination to illuminate legitimate and strategy activities for the security of biodiversity.

Besides, these gatherings frequently embrace mechanical advancements to upgrade their exploration abilities. The utilization of camera traps, satellite symbolism, and DNA investigation has become fundamental to checking untamed life populaces, figuring out biological systems, and distinguishing arising dangers. By utilizing logical aptitude and development, preservation bunches add to prove based dynamic in the field of untamed life protection.

Difficulties and Reactions

While natural life protection bunches assume a pivotal part in safeguarding biodiversity, they are not without difficulties and reactions. One outstanding test is the asset limitations looked by numerous associations. Restricted subsidizing and limit can hinder the scale and viability of protection endeavors. Also, concerns have been raised about the likely adverse consequence of some protection mediations on neighborhood networks, featuring the significance of taking on comprehensive and local area drove draws near.

Reactions have additionally been aimed at the hierarchical idea of some protection drives, with allegations of deficient commitment with nearby networks and lacking thought of native information. Finding some kind of harmony between preservation objectives and the necessities of nearby populaces stays a sensitive test for some untamed life protection gatherings.

Besides, the viability of specific protection systems, for example, hostage rearing and renewed introduction programs, has been a subject of discussion. While these endeavors have effectively saved a few animal categories from the edge of elimination, difficulties like hereditary variety, living space reasonableness, and the potential for infection transmission should be painstakingly explored.

Arising Patterns and Future Headings

1. **Innovation Mix and Large Information**

   The mix of innovation and the usage of large information are arising patterns in natural life preservation. Remote detecting, man-made brainpower, and information investigation empower more complete checking of environments and untamed life populaces. This mechanical shift upgrades the accuracy of protection endeavors, considering speedier reaction to arising dangers and more compelling designation of assets.

2. **Environmental Change Transformation Systems**

   Environmental change represents a critical danger to biodiversity, and untamed life preservation bunches are progressively integrating environmental change transformation systems into their tasks. This might include establishing environment strong natural surroundings, helping species in relocating to additional appropriate regions, and creating protection designs that think about the evolving environment.

3. **Corporate Associations for Preservation**

   Perceiving the effect of human exercises, including those of enterprises, on biodiversity, natural life protection bunches are manufacturing associations with organizations. These coordinated efforts intend to advance supportable practices, lessen the natural impression of enterprises, and add to the preservation of key living spaces.

4. **Comprehensive Protection and Native Freedoms**

   A rising accentuation on comprehensive protection approaches includes regarding and coordinating the freedoms and information on native people groups and nearby networks. This pattern perceives that fruitful protection endeavors should line up with the interests and yearnings of the people who live in nearness to natural life territories.

5. **One Wellbeing Approach**

The Coronavirus pandemic has highlighted the interconnectedness of human, creature, and natural wellbeing. Natural life protection bunches are taking on a One Wellbeing approach that perceives the connections between biodiversity, human prosperity, and the development of zoonotic sicknesses. This comprehensive viewpoint intends to address wellbeing challenges at the point of interaction of people, untamed life, and environments.

3.2 United Nations and Tiger Conservation Initiatives

Tigers, magnificent and jeopardized, stand at the very front of worldwide protection endeavors. Perceiving the basic significance of safeguarding these famous enormous felines and their natural surroundings, the Assembled Countries (UN) has been instrumental in leading tiger preservation drives. This paper investigates the job of the Assembled Countries in tiger preservation, featuring key drives, joint efforts, and the aggregate responsibility of the worldwide local area to shield these superb species.

1. **Foundation: The Predicament of Tigers**
   Tigers, when running across different living spaces in Asia, have confronted serious decreases in their populaces because of a juncture of dangers. Environment misfortune, poaching, human-untamed life clashes, and a lessening prey base have driven numerous tiger populaces to the edge of elimination. In light of this emergency, coordinated worldwide endeavors have been in progress to switch the downfall and guarantee the endurance of tigers in nature.
2. **The Assembled Countries and Natural Stewardship**
1. **Joined Countries Climate Program (UNEP)**

The Unified Countries Climate Program assumes a focal part in planning worldwide endeavors to address natural difficulties, including the preservation of biodiversity. UNEP gives a stage to countries to team up on natural issues and supports the improvement of worldwide strategies and systems.

While not exclusively centered around tigers, UNEP's more extensive command includes the interconnected issues that influence tiger environments and populaces.

III. Worldwide Tiger Drives: An UN-Drove Responsibility

1. **St. Petersburg Announcement on Tiger Preservation (2010)**
   A critical achievement in the UN-drove endeavors for tiger preservation was the St. Petersburg Statement, took on at the Worldwide Tiger Discussion in 2010. The statement put forth an aggressive objective to twofold the worldwide tiger populace by 2022, known as the TX2 objective. It united the heads of tiger-range nations, worldwide associations, and NGOs in an aggregate obligation to switch the downfall of wild tiger populaces.
   The St. Petersburg Statement perceived the desperation of tending to the different dangers looked by tigers and their territories. It underscored the requirement for a comprehensive methodology that incorporates living space insurance, hostile to poaching measures, and local area commitment. The statement denoted a memorable second, flagging a worldwide purpose to guarantee the endurance of one of the world's most notorious species.
2. **Worldwide Tiger Recuperation Program (GTRP)**
   Expanding on the St. Petersburg Statement, the Worldwide Tiger Recuperation Program (GTRP) was created to operationalize the responsibilities made by tiger-range nations. Sent off in 2010, the GTRP fills in as an exhaustive system for tiger protection, illustrating key procedures and activities expected to accomplish the aggressive TX2 objective.
   The GTRP centers around tending to the underlying drivers of tiger decline, including living space misfortune, poaching, and human-natural life clashes. It stresses the significance of connecting with nearby networks in preservation endeavors and advancing maintainable improvement rehearses that benefit the two

individuals and tigers. The GTRP addresses an organized and cooperative way to deal with tiger protection, with every tiger-range country fostering its own public tiger recuperation plan lined up with the general worldwide structure.

3. **Worldwide Tiger Day**

Perceiving the significance of bringing issues to light and gathering public help for tiger protection, the UN assigned July 29th as Worldwide Tiger Day. This yearly occasion fills in as a stage to feature the meaning of tiger preservation, exhibit accomplishments, and prepare endeavors to safeguard these sublime animals. Worldwide Tiger Day assumes a pivotal part in supporting worldwide consideration on tiger preservation and keeping up with the energy produced by the St. Petersburg Statement and the GTRP.

IV. Tiger Preservation at the Public Level: The Job of Tiger-Reach Nations

1. **Public Tiger Preservation Specialists**
Individual tiger-range nations assume a significant part in executing and propelling tiger protection drives. A considerable lot of these nations have laid out Public Tiger Preservation Specialists or comparable bodies liable for figuring out and executing public procedures for tiger protection.
For instance, India, with a critical piece of the world's wild tiger populace, has a devoted Public Tiger Protection Authority. This authority manages the execution of the nation's Venture Tiger, one of the longest-running and best tiger preservation programs all around the world. The task centers around territory insurance, hostile to poaching measures, and local area commitment.

2. **Natural life Asylums and Safeguarded Regions**

The foundation and compelling administration of untamed life asylums and safeguarded regions are major to tiger preservation. These regions act as shelters for tigers and their prey, giving undisturbed living spaces where these large felines can flourish. Tiger-range nations make progress toward extending and keeping up with such safeguarded regions, frequently fully supported by worldwide associations and subsidizing instruments.

The UN, through its different bodies and drives, supports and works with collaboration among tiger-range nations to reinforce their safeguarded region organizations. This cooperative methodology perceives that the endurance of tigers relies upon transboundary protection endeavors that rise above public lines.

V. Challenges in Tiger Protection

1. **Territory Fracture and Debasement**
The fracture and corruption of tiger living spaces stay huge difficulties. Fast urbanization, horticultural extension, and framework advancement frequently

bring about the discontinuity of once adjacent tiger scenes. Tending to these difficulties requires the security of existing environments as well as the rebuilding and availability of scenes to consider the development of tiger populaces.

2. **Poaching and Unlawful Natural life Exchange**

   In spite of expanded endeavors to battle poaching and the unlawful natural life exchange, these dangers endure. Interest for tiger parts in customary medication and the underground market keeps on driving poaching exercises. Worldwide cooperation, reinforced policing, mindfulness crusades are fundamental parts of the battle against poaching.

3. **Human-Natural life Clashes**

As human populaces venture into tiger environments, clashes among people and tigers raise. Tigers might go after domesticated animals, prompting retaliatory killings by networks. Successful procedures for relieving human-untamed life clashes include local area commitment, the advancement of elective livelihoods, and the execution of measures to safeguard the two individuals and tigers.

VI. Examples of overcoming adversity and Progress in Tiger Preservation

1. **India's Task Tiger**

   India's Task Tiger, sent off in 1973, remains as one of the best tiger preservation drives around the world. The task, which plans to safeguard basic tiger natural surroundings and guarantee a suitable populace of wild tigers, has prompted a critical expansion in tiger numbers in India. Protection systems under Venture Tiger incorporate living space safeguarding, against poaching endeavors, and local area association.

2. **Bhutan's Protection Accomplishments**

Bhutan, a tiger-range country, has taken striking steps in tiger protection. The country's obligation to keeping up with woodland cover and the execution of local area based protection drives have added to the progress of Bhutan's tiger preservation endeavors. The cooperation between the public authority, nearby networks, and global associations has been critical to Bhutan's accomplishments in safeguarding its tiger populaces.

VII. Future Headings and Worldwide Coordinated effort

1. **Inventive Protection Advances**

   Headways in innovation, including the utilization of camera traps, satellite following, and information examination, offer new roads for tiger protection. These instruments upgrade observing capacities, give important information to investigate, and add to more powerful protection methodologies. The UN, through its help for mechanical development, adds to the worldwide work to use state of the art arrangements in tiger preservation.

2. **Financial Motivations for Protection**
Perceiving the interconnectedness of preservation and manageable turn of events, future headings in tiger protection might include investigating monetary motivations for nearby networks. The UN can assume a part in advancing models that exhibit the monetary benefit of safeguarding sound biological systems, including those possessed by tigers. Drives that connect preservation with the travel industry, economical horticulture, and biological system administrations can add to long haul achievement.

3. **Improved Worldwide Cooperation**

As tiger preservation is intrinsically a transboundary issue, upgraded global coordinated effort stays significant. The UN can keep on working with discoursed, give a stage to information trade, and prepare assets to help cooperative ventures. Reinforcing associations between tiger-range nations, worldwide associations, and NGOs will be fundamental for accomplishing the objectives illustrated in the St. Petersburg Statement and the Worldwide Tiger Recuperation Program.

3.3 Collaborative Projects Across Borders
Cooperative ventures across borders address a strong power in tending to worldwide difficulties and encouraging positive change. In a world interconnected by innovation, exchange, and shared natural worries, global cooperation has become fundamental. This exposition investigates the meaning of cooperative tasks across borders, their effect on different areas, and the potential for molding an additional interconnected and reasonable future.

1. **Presentation: The Basic of Worldwide Coordinated effort**
In a time set apart by shared difficulties, for example, environmental change, general wellbeing emergencies, and biodiversity misfortune, the requirement for cooperative activities across borders has never been more basic. Global joint effort rises above political limits, utilizing aggregate mastery, assets, and viewpoints to handle complex issues that resist one-sided arrangements.

2. **Natural Preservation and Biodiversity Security**

1. **Transboundary Preservation Drives**
Natural preservation frequently requires a cross-line approach, especially while managing biological systems that length numerous nations. Cooperative tasks in this domain expect to safeguard biodiversity, safeguard basic territories, and address the effects of environmental change. The Amazon Rainforest, for instance, ranges a few South American nations, requiring cooperative endeavors to battle deforestation and advance economical land use.
Drives, for example, the "Biosphere Stores" assigned by UNESCO epitomize

cooperative tasks that rise above public lines. These stores expect to accommodate the preservation of biodiversity with manageable turn of events, cultivating global collaboration in the assurance of regular regions.

2. **Worldwide Environment Arrangements**

The Paris Understanding, a milestone worldwide environment accord, highlights the meaning of cooperative undertakings in relieving environmental change.

Uniting countries from around the world, the understanding commits nations to restrict a dangerous atmospheric devation and adjust to its belongings. The cooperative idea of such arrangements recognizes that environmental change is a common test that requests brought together activity.

Cooperative activities connected with environmental change incorporate joint exploration attempts, innovation move drives, and limit building programs. These endeavors mean to upgrade flexibility, diminish ozone harming substance discharges, and speed up the change to a maintainable, low-carbon future.

III. General Wellbeing and Infectious prevention

1. **Pandemic Readiness and Reaction**

The Coronavirus pandemic featured the significance of cooperative ventures in general wellbeing. The fast spread of the infection across borders required worldwide participation in research, immunization improvement, and the fair appropriation of clinical assets. Drives like COVAX, a worldwide immunization sharing project, represent cooperative endeavors to guarantee that antibodies arrive at populaces around the world.

Cooperative exploration projects including researchers and medical care experts from various nations play had a vital impact in grasping the infection, creating diagnostics, and distinguishing compelling therapies. The World Wellbeing Association (WHO) fills in as a critical facilitator of worldwide cooperation in general wellbeing, organizing reactions to wellbeing crises and elevating impartial admittance to medical care assets.

IV. Exchange and Financial Turn of events

1. **Worldwide Economic accords**

Cooperative undertakings in the domain of exchange and financial improvement expect to encourage flourishing by separating boundaries to business. Economic alliance, like the North American International alliance (NAFTA) and the Complete and Moderate Arrangement for Transoceanic Organization (CPTPP), make systems for monetary participation among nations.

These arrangements advance the free progression of labor and products, invigorate monetary development, and improve the seriousness of partaking countries. Cooperative financial activities likewise incorporate framework improvement, joint speculation drives, and innovation move, adding to shared success and security.

V. Innovation and Advancement

1. Worldwide Exploration Joint efforts

In the area of innovation and development, cooperative ventures across borders are driving headways that benefit humankind overall. Logical examination, especially in regions like space investigation, molecule physical science, and clinical leap forwards, frequently includes worldwide coordinated effort. The Huge Hadron Collider at CERN and the Worldwide Space Station are instances of enormous scope cooperative undertakings that unite researchers, specialists, and assets from various nations.

Cooperation in innovation stretches out to the sharing of information, open-source improvement, and joint drives to address worldwide difficulties. Stages like the Human Genome Venture, which planned the whole human genome, represent how worldwide coordinated effort can speed up logical advancement.

VI. Difficulties and Contemplations in Cooperative Activities Across Lines

1. **Variety of Partners**
   Cooperative activities across borders include different partners with fluctuating needs, viewpoints, and interests. Arranging arrangements and guaranteeing impartial investment can be mind boggling, requiring viable correspondence and strategy. Finding some kind of harmony between the interests of various countries and partners is pivotal for the achievement and supportability of cooperative drives.

2. **Political and International Elements**
   Political contemplations and international strains can affect the viability of cooperative tasks. Changes in conciliatory relations, exchange debates, and clashes between countries can present difficulties to continuous drives. Exploring these elements requires talented strategy and a guarantee to exchange and collaboration.

3. **Asset Designation and Subsidizing**
   Cooperative tasks frequently require huge monetary assets, and getting subsidizing from various sources can be a test. Guaranteeing fair and straightforward asset distribution, as well as tending to abberations in monetary commitments, is fundamental for the drawn out progress of cooperative undertakings.

4. **Adjusting to Social Contrasts**

Social subtleties and contrasts in administrative structures can present difficulties in cooperative activities. Understanding and regarding social variety is critical to cultivating compelling correspondence, building trust, and guaranteeing that undertakings are executed in a way that is delicate to nearby settings.

VII. Future Headings: Cultivating a Cooperative Worldwide People group

1. **Bridling Advanced Availability**

   The computerized age has changed the scene of coordinated effort, making it more straightforward for people, associations, and countries to interface and work together. Computerized stages work with ongoing correspondence, information sharing, and cooperative critical thinking. Embracing computerized network can improve the effectiveness and reach of cooperative activities across borders.

2. **Instruction and Information Trade**

   Advancing instruction and information trade is significant for building a cooperative worldwide local area. Drives that work with understudy trades, joint examination projects, and worldwide organizations in training add to a common pool of information and encourage shared understanding.

3. **Engaging Common Society and Grassroots Developments**

   Cooperation isn't restricted to legislative or institutional endeavors; common society and grassroots developments assume an essential part. Engaging neighborhood networks, NGOs, and promotion gatherings to team up across borders improves the effect of aggregate activity. These gatherings frequently offer one of a kind points of view and arrangements of real value, adding to additional comprehensive and economical results.

4. **Tending to Worldwide Imbalances**

Cooperative tasks ought to focus on tending to worldwide disparities, both inside and between countries. Endeavors to overcome any barrier among created and emerging nations, advance civil rights, and address foundational disparities are vital to building an additional equitable and cooperative world.

VIII.Toward a Cooperative Future

Cooperative undertakings across borders epitomize the aggregate desires of mankind to address shared difficulties and fabricate a superior future. From natural preservation and general wellbeing to financial turn of events and mechanical development, worldwide cooperation is a main impetus for positive change.

As we explore an inexorably interconnected world, encouraging cooperation isn't simply a decision yet a need. The difficulties we face — whether ecological, social, or monetary — are worldwide in nature, rising above borders and requesting aggregate arrangements. By embracing the soul of joint effort, countries, associations, and people can intensify their effect, making a stronger and supportable world for a long time into the future.

Chapter 4

Technology And Innovation in Conservation

Preservation, notwithstanding raising natural difficulties, has entered another period impelled by innovation and advancement. The combination of state of the art advancements with conventional protection rehearses is reclassifying the way that we approach natural stewardship. This exhaustive investigation dives into the bunch ways innovation and development are changing preservation endeavors around the world. From information driven protection techniques and remote detecting to man-made brainpower and local area commitment, this article navigates the scene of innovation's effect on safeguarding biodiversity and supporting our planet.

II. Information Driven Preservation Methodologies

1. **Huge Information Examination in Biodiversity Observing**

The approach of large information examination has upset biodiversity checking and natural exploration. Huge datasets, gathered through different sources like satellite symbolism, camera traps, and sensor organizations, are handled to separate significant experiences. AI calculations examine designs in species conveyance, relocation, and conduct, furnishing preservationists with a more profound comprehension of biological systems.

1. **Model: eBird and Resident Science**

Stages like eBird represent the force of resident science and huge information in ornithological exploration. Bird watchers overall contribute their perceptions, making a tremendous data set that assists scientists with following bird populaces, movement examples, and reactions to natural changes. This democratization of information assortment improves the accuracy of preservation endeavors.

B. Satellite Innovation for Environment Checking

Satellite innovation offers an elevated perspective of Earth, empowering continuous checking of living spaces and scenes. From deforestation and land-use changes to the effect of environmental change, satellites give significant information to confirm based dynamic in protection.

1. Model: Worldwide Timberland Watch

Worldwide Timberland Watch uses satellite symbolism to screen deforestation in close constant. By joining trend setting innovation with open-access information, this stage engages state run administrations, NGOs, and neighborhood networks to track and battle unlawful logging, land infringements, and different dangers to woods biological systems.

III. Remote Detecting and Geospatial Innovations

1. UAVs (Automated Flying Vehicles) for Accuracy Preservation

Automated Flying Vehicles, regularly known as robots, have arisen as major advantages in preservation. Furnished with cameras and sensors, drones give high-goal symbolism and information for exact planning, environment evaluation, and natural life checking.

1. Model: Checking Marine Stores

Drones are utilized to screen marine holds and survey the wellbeing of coral reefs. By catching top notch pictures and recordings, specialists can examine changes in reef structures, distinguish coral fading, and assess the viability of preservation estimates in safeguarding marine biodiversity.

B. Geographic Data Framework (GIS) Applications

Geographic Data Framework (GIS) innovation works with the reconciliation and examination of spatial information, offering an amazing asset for preservation arranging and the board. GIS applications empower moderates to plan biodiversity areas of interest, plan safeguarded regions, and survey the network of environments.

1. Model: Preservation Arranging in the Amazon

GIS is broadly utilized in the Amazon rainforest for preservation arranging. By planning biodiversity, land use, and possible dangers, progressives can distinguish need regions for security, directing strategies that offset natural protection with feasible turn of events.

IV. Man-made reasoning (artificial intelligence) in Preservation

1. **AI for Species Distinguishing proof**

AI calculations, a subset of man-made consciousness, are progressively utilized for species distinguishing proof. PC vision models can break down pictures and sounds, computerizing the most common way of distinguishing greenery in nature.

1. **Model: computer based intelligence controlled Camera Traps**

Computer based intelligence is applied to camera trap information to distinguish and group creatures caught in pictures. This speeds up the examination of immense datasets, permitting analysts to screen natural life populaces, track individual creatures, and survey the effect of ecological changes all the more productively.

B. Prescient Demonstrating for Preservation Arranging

Computer based intelligence driven prescient demonstrating expects the outcomes of different preservation situations. By breaking down authentic information and ecological factors, these models figure possible future results, helping moderates in formulating proactive systems.

1. **Model: Foreseeing Species Weakness to Environmental Change**

Man-made intelligence calculations examine environment information, living space attributes, and species characteristics to anticipate how various species could answer environmental change. This data focuses on protection activities for species generally defenseless against moving natural circumstances.

V. Preservation Hereditary qualities and Genomic Innovations

1. **DNA Barcoding for Species ID**

DNA barcoding includes sequencing a short DNA section to recognize species. This atomic strategy is significant for distinguishing organic entities, particularly in complex environments where customary recognizable proof techniques may challenge.

1. **Model: Scanner tag of Life Information Frameworks**

Projects like the Scanner tag of Life Information Frameworks keep up with broad DNA standardized identification libraries. These data sets help in species ID, combatting unlawful natural life exchange, and guaranteeing the validness of organic examples in protection research.

B. Genomic Apparatuses for Populace The executives

Progressions in genomic advances give bits of knowledge into the hereditary variety, wellbeing, and versatility of populaces. Preservation geneticists use methods like cutting edge sequencing to illuminate populace the board procedures and alleviate inbreeding.

1. Model: Concentrating on Imperiled Species

For jeopardized species like the cheetah, genomic instruments assist with surveying hereditary variety and distinguish key populaces for protection intercession. This data guides rearing projects and territory the executives to guarantee the drawn out reasonability of the species.

VI. Innovation Empowered People group Commitment

1. Versatile Innovation for Preservation Effort

Versatile innovation, including cell phones and applications, enables nearby networks to take part in preservation endeavors effectively. These devices work with data sharing, announcing of ecological issues, and constant correspondence among networks and preservation associations.

1. Model: Savvy Protection Application

The Spatial Observing and Revealing Device (Savvy) is an application utilized for watching and checking safeguarded regions. Officers and local area individuals can report natural life sightings, criminal operations, and dangers, improving the proficiency of protection watches.

B. Computer generated Reality (VR) and Expanded Reality (AR) for Schooling

Virtual and expanded reality innovations make vivid instructive encounters, cultivating a more profound comprehension of environments and untamed life. These advancements are used in preservation schooling to bring issues to light and rouse ecological stewardship.

1. Model: Augmented Experience Nature Stores

Computer generated reality encounters permit people to investigate mimicked nature saves, focusing on the magnificence and significance of safeguarded regions. This virtual commitment improves ecological mindfulness and energizes support for preservation drives.

VII. Challenges and Moral Contemplations

1. **Moral Utilization of Innovation in Protection**
   The fast reconciliation of innovation in protection raises moral contemplations. Issues like information security, the expected abuse of simulated intelligence in natural life reconnaissance, and the potentially negative side-effects of hereditary mediations require cautious moral examination.

2. **Access and Value in Innovation Reception**
   Guaranteeing fair admittance to innovation is vital for the outcome of protection drives. Variations in innovation reception, especially in creating locales, should be addressed to abstain from compounding existing imbalances in preservation results.

3. **Mechanical Reliance and Human Abilities**

4. While innovation improves preservation endeavors, there is a gamble of over-reliance on mechanical arrangements. It is vital for offset mechanical devices with conventional biological information and human abilities, recognizing the corresponding jobs they play in successful preservation.

   VIII. Contextual analyses: Mechanical Developments in real life

1. **Contextual investigation 1: The Snow Panther Trust's Camera Traps**
   The Snow Panther Trust utilizes camera traps outfitted with cutting edge sensors and man-made intelligence to screen subtle snow panthers right at home. This innovation empowers specialists to accumulate significant information on snow panther populaces, conduct, and communications with nearby networks.

2. **Contextual investigation 2: Moment Identify - Acoustic Observing for Frogs**

   The Moment Distinguish framework utilizes acoustic observing to identify the presence of jeopardized frogs continuously. By dissecting frog calls through AI calculations, this innovation helps scientists in surveying frog populaces and creating designated protection procedures.

   IX. Future Bearings: Mechanical Outskirts in Preservation

1. **Joining of Blockchain for Protection**
   Blockchain innovation, known for its straightforwardness and security, holds expected in protection. Its application in production network checking, straightforward exchanges, and secure information sharing can battle unlawful untamed life exchange and improve trust in protection endeavors.

2. **High level Sensors and Web of Things (IoT)**
   The multiplication of cutting edge sensors and IoT gadgets in far off regions works with continuous observing of ecological boundaries. From

following environment changes to checking natural life conduct, these advances offer unrivaled experiences into biological systems.

3. **Quantum Registering for Complex Biological Displaying**
The computational requests of mind boggling biological displaying can be met with the appearance of quantum processing. Quantum calculations might upset how researchers mimic environmental cycles, empowering more precise expectations and situation examinations.

4. **Innovative Answers for Obtrusive Species The executives**

Obtrusive species represent a critical danger to biodiversity. Trend setting innovations, for example, quality altering devices like CRISPR, offer possible answers for overseeing intrusive species and reestablishing environmental equilibrium.

4.1 Advances in Monitoring and Tracking Tigers

Tigers, sublime and imperiled, stand as famous images of the world's biodiversity. With their populaces under danger because of natural surroundings misfortune, poaching, and human-untamed life clashes, successful checking and following are pivotal for guaranteeing the endurance of these grand enormous felines. This article investigates the advances in innovation and systems utilized in checking and following tigers. From conventional strategies to state of the art advances, the aggregate endeavors to defend and reestablish tiger populaces exhibit the convergence of preservation and development.

II. Customary Observing Techniques

1. Impression Following and Sign Studies

Customary following techniques depend on the mastery of field scholars and moderates who track tigers through their impressions and signs in nature. Impression following, otherwise called pugmark following, includes recognizing and investigating the prints left by tigers. Sign reviews remember reading up scratches for trees, defecation, and different markings to decide the presence, conduct, and strength of tigers.

1. Limits of Conventional Following

While these techniques give important bits of knowledge, they are work serious, tedious, and subject to the expertise of the tracker. Besides, they offer restricted data about the tiger's more extensive natural setting.

III. Radio-Telemetry and Nabbing

1. Early Radio-Telemetry

The presentation of radio-telemetry reformed natural life observing during the twentieth 100 years. Tigers were fitted with radio collars furnished with transmitters, empowering specialists to follow their developments. This innovation essentially improved the capacity to figure out the spatial biology and conduct of tigers.

1. Difficulties of Early Radio-Telemetry

Notwithstanding, early radio-telemetry had impediments, including the massiveness of collars, restricted battery duration, and the requirement for analysts to be in nearness to the apprehended tigers for following. Furthermore, the information gathered was much of the time restricted to area data.

IV. Satellite Following and GPS Innovation

1. Development of Satellite Following

Headways in satellite following and GPS innovation denoted an extraordinary stage in tiger checking. Satellite collars, outfitted with GPS gadgets, permitted analysts to follow tigers continuously from a distance. The mix of satellite innovation into protection endeavors extended the scale and proficiency of observing, giving more exhaustive information on tiger developments.

1. Continuous Information and Remote Checking

Satellite following defeated the constraints of early radio-telemetry by giving ongoing information and empowering specialists to screen tigers across huge scenes from a distance. This innovation works with the following of tigers in testing landscapes and out of reach regions, offering a more thorough comprehension of their way of behaving and territory use.

B. GPS Collars and Development Biology

GPS innovation in collars gives nitty gritty data about the development biology of tigers. Scientists can break down information on home reach, living space inclinations, and halls utilized for relocation. This information is priceless for preservation arranging and the ID of basic living spaces that require assurance.

1. Model: Siberian Tigers in Russia

In Russia, GPS collars have been instrumental in following Siberian tigers. The information gathered uncovered their broad home reaches, relocation designs, and the significance of keeping up with enormous, interconnected scenes for the endurance of this subspecies.

V. Camera Traps and Visual Observing

1. Reforming Natural life Reconnaissance

Camera traps have arisen as integral assets for checking tigers and other untamed life. These movement enacted cameras catch pictures and recordings when set off by the development of creatures. Sent decisively in tiger territories, camera traps give non-nosy and ceaseless observation.

1. Benefits of Camera Traps

Camera traps beat the impediments of direct human perception and proposition an abundance of data. They give visual recognizable proof of individual tigers in view of novel coat examples and markings, gauge populace densities, and proposition experiences into conduct, regenerative achievement, and communications with different species.

B. AI and Robotized Investigation

Propels in AI and man-made reasoning have changed the examination of camera trap information. Robotized acknowledgment calculations can process immense datasets, recognize individual tigers, and sort ways of behaving. This mechanical jump improves the proficiency and precision of camera trap studies.

1. Model: The Depiction Serengeti Task

The Preview Serengeti project, using AI calculations, permits resident researchers to order creatures caught in huge number of camera trap pictures. This cooperative methodology supports observing tigers as well as draws in general society in natural life preservation.

VI. Painless Hereditary Observing

1. DNA Investigation for Populace Evaluation

Painless hereditary checking includes gathering DNA tests from tiger scat, hair, or spit. Hereditary investigation permits scientists to distinguish individual tigers, gauge populace sizes, survey hereditary variety, and grasp the elements of tiger populaces.

1. Protection Hereditary qualities and Inbreeding Aversion

Hereditary checking is critical for resolving issues of inbreeding, guaranteeing the drawn out reasonability of tiger populaces. Preservation geneticists utilize this information to illuminate rearing projects, movement endeavors, and natural surroundings the board procedures.

B. Challenges and Moral Contemplations

While harmless hereditary checking is an amazing asset, it presents difficulties, including the requirement for modern lab offices, moral contemplations connected with test assortment, and the possible effect on individual tigers. Finding some kind of harmony between the advantages and moral contemplations is fundamental for mindful preservation rehearses.

VII. Acoustic Observing and Soundscapes

1. Bioacoustics for Tiger Recognizable proof

Acoustic observing, using bioacoustics, includes recording and dissecting the vocalizations of tigers. Every tiger has a novel vocal mark, permitting scientists to distinguish people and screen their presence in a space.

1. Model: Tiger Vocalizations in Nepal

In Nepal, specialists utilize acoustic checking to distinguish individual tigers by their thunders. This non-meddling strategy supplements other checking procedures and adds to a more exhaustive comprehension of tiger populaces.

VIII. Difficulties and Future Bearings

1. Choker Impediments and Creature Government assistance

While following collars have been instrumental, challenges continue. The utilization of collars raises worries about the prosperity of individual tigers, including possible pressure, wounds, or obstruction with normal way of behaving. Constant headways in collar plan and materials expect to address these worries.

2. Coordinating Numerous Advancements

The fate of tiger observing lies in coordinating different advancements to make a comprehensive comprehension of tiger environment. Joining information from GPS collars, camera traps, hereditary investigations, and acoustic observing gives a thorough image of tiger populaces, ways of behaving, and environmental necessities.

3. **The Job of Resident Science and Local area Contribution**
Drawing in neighborhood networks and resident researchers in checking endeavors cultivates a feeling of pride and obligation. Local area based observing projects upgrade information assortment as well as add to preservation mindfulness and schooling.

4. **Tending to Arising Dangers**

As innovation advances, so do the dangers to tigers. The unlawful utilization of innovation, for example, drones for poaching or unsettling influence, presents new difficulties. Protection endeavors should adjust to these dangers by integrating against poaching advancements and observation measures.

IX. Contextual investigations: Fruitful Execution of Observing Innovations

1. **Contextual investigation 1: The Sundarbans Tiger Task**
In the Sundarbans mangrove woods, camera traps and satellite following have been instrumental in checking Bengal tigers. Scientists utilize this innovation to figure out tiger developments in a difficult and dynamic environment, illuminating protection systems for this remarkable populace.

2. **Contextual investigation 2: The Russian Far East Tiger Observing System**

The Russian Far East Tiger Checking Project uses a mix of GPS collars and camera traps to screen Amur tigers. The information gathered has been critical for figuring out their way of behaving, distinguishing key environments, and executing preservation measures to safeguard this imperiled subspecies.

4.2 Use of Drones and Remote Sensing in Habitat Protection
The heightening dangers to normal environments and biodiversity request imaginative and proficient preservation techniques. In this mechanical time, the mix of robots and remote detecting has arisen as an integral asset for natural surroundings security. This paper investigates the groundbreaking effect of robots and remote detecting advancements on protection endeavors, zeroing in on their applications, benefits, and commitments to shielding biological systems.

II. Grasping Remote Detecting

1. **Outline of Remote Detecting**

Remote detecting includes the assortment and translation of data about the World's surface without direct actual contact. Sensors on satellites, airplane, or robots catch information, giving significant experiences into land cover, vegetation wellbeing, and changes in the climate.

1. Multispectral and Hyperspectral Imaging

Remote detecting uses multispectral and hyperspectral imaging to catch data across various frequencies. This empowers the recognizable proof of explicit highlights, for example, vegetation types, water bodies, and land use designs.

B. Satellite-Based Remote Detecting

Satellite-based remote detecting offers a wide-scale point of view, covering broad regions at customary spans. Satellites outfitted with different sensors catch information that guides in observing enormous scope ecological changes, deforestation, and environment wellbeing.

1. Benefits and Constraints

While satellite-based remote detecting is significant for wide scale appraisals, it might have limits regarding spatial goal and return to recurrence. This is where drones, with their adaptability and accuracy, assume a critical part.

III. Drones in Protection: A Game-Changing Innovation

1. The Ascent of Protection Robots

Preservation drones, or Automated Airborne Vehicles (UAVs), have reformed the manner in which traditionalists approach territory security. These little, dexterous airplanes furnished with sensors give high-goal symbolism, taking into consideration itemized observing and examination of explicit regions.

1. Key Highlights of Preservation Robots

High Spatial Goal: Robots catch high-goal pictures, empowering point by point investigations of environment highlights.

Adaptability and Mobility: Robots can explore testing landscapes, arriving at regions that are challenging to access by customary means.

Cost-Viability: Contrasted with monitored airplane, drones offer a more financially savvy answer for continuous and designated information assortment.

B. Utilizations of Robots in Environment Security

1. Observing Deforestation and Land Use Changes

Drones are instrumental in checking deforestation and land use changes in close ongoing. High-goal pictures give exact information on the degree of deforestation, unlawful logging exercises, and infringements into safeguarded regions.

2. **Untamed life Checking and Hostile to Poaching Endeavors**
   Drones improve natural life observing by giving a 10,000 foot perspective of territories. They are especially viable in enemy of poaching endeavors, empowering officers to watch huge regions proficiently and distinguish expected dangers to untamed life.

3. **Planning and Protection Arranging**
   Drones support territory planning and protection arranging by making nitty gritty, modern guides. This guides in distinguishing basic natural surroundings, arranging reclamation projects, and executing measures to moderate the effect of human exercises.

4. **Biological system Wellbeing Evaluation**

Evaluating the strength of biological systems is critical for environment insurance. Drones furnished with different sensors can catch information on vegetation wellbeing, water quality, and other natural boundaries, adding to extensive environment observing.

IV. Remote Detecting Innovations for Living space Assurance

1. **Satellite-Based Remote Detecting**

Satellites furnished with cutting edge sensors contribute essentially to territory insurance. From checking huge scope land cover changes to evaluating the effect of environmental change, satellite-based remote detecting gives a worldwide viewpoint on natural elements.

1. **Worldwide Inclusion and Enormous Scope Observing**
   Satellites offer worldwide inclusion, making them essential for observing changes in biodiversity and environments on a planetary scale. They give significant information to worldwide preservation endeavors and the evaluation of worldwide biodiversity areas of interest.

2. **Persistent Checking of Environments**

Satellites empower persistent checking of environments over the long run. This longitudinal information is fundamental for figuring out patterns, recognizing dangers, and planning versatile preservation systems.

B. Hyperspectral Imaging

Hyperspectral imaging, both from satellites and robots, catches a great many frequencies past the noticeable range. This itemized otherworldly data supports the distinguishing proof of explicit vegetation types, stress pointers, and natural varieties.

1. Vegetation Investigation and Wellbeing Observing

Hyperspectral imaging works with exact vegetation investigation, permitting progressives to evaluate plant wellbeing, distinguish intrusive species, and recognize early indications of stress or infection. This data is basic for environment security and reclamation endeavors.

C. LiDAR Innovation

Light Discovery and Running (LiDAR) innovation utilizes laser shafts to quantify removes and make point by point, three-layered guides of landscape. LiDAR-prepared robots and airplane give exact geographical data, improving living space evaluation and checking.

1. Territory Planning and Natural surroundings Construction

LiDAR innovation is especially important for planning territory and understanding natural surroundings structure. It can portray rise changes, recognize microhabitats, and help with surveying the appropriateness of regions for specific species.

V. Benefits of Robots and Remote Detecting in Territory Assurance

1. **Fast Information Assortment and Examination**
   Robots and remote detecting advancements empower fast information assortment and examination. Traditionalists can acquire convenient data on natural surroundings changes, empowering quick reactions to arising dangers or aggravations.

2. **Financially savvy Observing**
   Contrasted with customary techniques or monitored airplane, drones offer a savvy answer for territory checking. Their moderateness and capacity to cover designated regions pursue them a functional decision for preservation associations with restricted assets.

3. **Improved Accuracy and Detail**
   The high-goal symbolism gave by rambles permits to improved accuracy and definite examination. Traditionalists can focus in on unambiguous areas of interest, distinguish individual plants or creatures, and screen changes with a degree of detail that was beforehand impossible.

4. **Adaptability in Sending**

Drones are profoundly adaptable in their arrangement, fit for exploring testing landscapes and getting to remote or out of reach regions. This adaptability is pivotal for observing environments that might be challenging to arrive at through customary means.

VI. Difficulties and Contemplations

1. **Administrative Difficulties**
   The utilization of robots for preservation intentions is dependent upon different guidelines. Exploring lawful systems, getting grants, and guaranteeing consistence with flight guidelines can be trying for protection associations.

2. **Specialized Constraints**
   While robots and remote detecting innovations offer various benefits, they additionally have specialized constraints. Factors like battery duration, payload limit, and antagonistic atmospheric conditions can influence the adequacy of information assortment.

3. **Moral Contemplations**
   The utilization of innovation in territory security raises moral contemplations, including protection concerns, the expected aggravation to untamed life, and the effect on nearby networks.
   Capable and moral practices should be focused on in the arrangement of robots and remote detecting.

4. **Joining with Conventional Information**

   While innovation assumes a pivotal part, it ought to supplement instead of supplant conventional natural information. Incorporating the experiences of neighborhood networks and native individuals is fundamental for comprehensive territory assurance.

VII. Contextual analyses: Effective Execution of Robots and Remote Detecting

1. **Contextual analysis 1: Preservation Robots in Sumatra**
   Preservation associations in Sumatra have effectively involved robots to screen unlawful logging exercises in basic orangutan territories. The robots give constant data, empowering specialists to make a prompt move against deforestation.

2. **Contextual analysis 2: Remote Detecting in the Amazon Rainforest**

   Satellite-based remote detecting has been utilized in the Amazon rainforest to screen deforestation and evaluate the effect of human exercises. The nonstop observing worked with by satellites adds to worldwide endeavors to ration this imperative environment.

VIII. Future Headings: Mechanical Boondocks in Environment Assurance

1. **Man-made reasoning for Robotized Examination**

   The reconciliation of computerized reasoning (artificial intelligence) into robot and remote detecting information investigation holds tremendous potential. Simulated intelligence calculations can robotize the recognizable proof of living space changes, species dispersions, and expected dangers, smoothing out the checking system.

2. **Joint effort and Information Sharing**

   The fate of natural surroundings security lies in upgraded joint effort and information sharing. Laying out worldwide organizations that associate protection associations, specialists, and state run administrations can work with the trading of data and assets for more compelling preservation methodologies.

3. **Advancement in Sensor Advances**

   Proceeded with development in sensor advancements, remembering progressions for hyperspectral imaging, LiDAR, and warm imaging, will additionally upgrade the capacities of robots and remote detecting in living space security. These developments will empower more extensive and nuanced observing of biological systems.

4. **Public Commitment and Schooling**

Outfitting the force of innovation for natural surroundings insurance ought to be joined by endeavors to draw in the general population and bring issues to light. Instructive projects that feature the job of robots and remote detecting in preservation can encourage a feeling of obligation and natural stewardship.

4.3 Genetic Research for Population Management

Hereditary examination has turned into a foundation in the field of protection, offering an accuracy way to deal with populace the board. As biodiversity faces phenomenal difficulties, for example, living space misfortune, environmental change, and human-natural life clashes, understanding and utilizing hereditary data is essential for the economical administration and endurance of jeopardized species. This exposition investigates the meaning of hereditary examination in populace the executives, its applications, challenges, and the groundbreaking effect it has on protection techniques.

II. Significance of Hereditary Variety

1. **The Job of Hereditary Variety**

Hereditary variety is the foundation of an animal groups' versatility and strength. A different genetic stock empowers populaces to develop, adjust to evolving conditions, and endure dangers like infections. It is an essential part of the drawn out endurance and strength of any species.

1. Hereditary Variety and Biological system Working

Past the endurance of individual species, hereditary variety adds to the general working and strength of biological systems. It improves natural solidness, upholds species associations, and advances biological system flexibility even with ecological aggravations.

III. Utilizations of Hereditary Exploration in Protection

1. Distinguishing Remarkable Populaces

Hereditary examination permits researchers to distinguish novel populaces inside an animal types. This is especially vital for species with divided living spaces, as particular populaces might confront various dangers and require custom fitted protection procedures.

1. Model: Cheetahs in Namibia

In Namibia, hereditary examinations uncovered that cheetahs are separated into unmistakable populaces with restricted quality stream. This data is indispensable for planning protection designs that address the particular necessities and difficulties looked by every populace.

B. Surveying Hereditary Wellbeing

Hereditary exploration gives experiences into the strength of populaces by evaluating variables like inbreeding, loss of hereditary inconstancy, and the presence of hurtful hereditary transformations. This data guides protectionists in settling on informed choices to forestall the adverse consequences of diminished hereditary wellbeing.

1. Inbreeding Melancholy and Diminished Wellness

Inbreeding melancholy, an outcome of mating between firmly related people, can prompt decreased wellness and conceptive achievement. Hereditary exploration distinguishes populaces in danger of inbreeding melancholy and illuminates techniques to moderate its belongings.

C. Protection Rearing Projects

Hereditary data is urgent in overseeing hostage rearing projects. Via cautiously choosing people for rearing in view of their hereditary similarity and variety, traditionalists plan to keep up with solid and hereditarily vigorous populaces for expected renewed introduction into nature.

1. Job of Zoos in Preservation Hereditary qualities

Zoos assume a vital part in preservation hereditary qualities by taking part in reproducing programs that focus on hereditary variety. These projects add to the ex-situ protection of imperiled species and go about as repositories for hereditary material.

D. Movement and Support

Movement includes moving people starting with one populace then onto the next, and hereditary examination guarantees the progress of such endeavors. Understanding the hereditary cosmetics of source and beneficiary populaces is critical for keeping up with variety and staying away from unfortunate results.

1. Renewed introduction of Wolves in Yellowstone Public Park

The renewed introduction of wolves to Yellowstone Public Park included thinking about hereditary variety. Wolves from various source populaces were acquainted with upgrade hereditary changeability and work on the possibilities of a fruitful renewed introduction.

E. Observing Populace Elements

Hereditary markers act as useful assets for observing changes in populace elements over the long run. Through strategies like DNA profiling and finger-printing, specialists can follow people, survey populace measures, and recognize the effect of protection mediations.

1. Headways in Harmless Hereditary Testing

Painless hereditary testing, like gathering DNA from defecation, hair, or plumes, has progressed checking abilities without the requirement for direct contact with untamed life. This negligibly obtrusive methodology is especially advantageous for subtle or jeopardized species.

IV. Challenges in Hereditary Exploration for Protection

1. Restricted Assets and Financing

Directing hereditary examination, particularly thorough genome sequencing, requires critical assets and financing. Numerous protection projects face difficulties in getting the essential monetary help for top to bottom hereditary examinations.

2. **Moral Contemplations**

Hereditary examination frequently includes gathering tests straightforwardly from wild populaces, raising moral contemplations about expected aggravations and effects on people or environments. Finding some kind of harmony between research needs and moral untamed life rehearses is a continuous test.

3. **Absence of Far reaching Information**

For some species, far reaching hereditary information might need. Deficient hereditary data thwarts the capacity to settle on very much educated choices, particularly in situations where desperation is principal, for example, with basically imperiled species.

4. **Adjusting Ex-Situ and In-Situ Preservation**

The harmony between ex-situ (hostage) and in-situ (wild) preservation approaches presents difficulties. While protection reproducing programs add to hereditary variety, keeping up with the normal ways of behaving and biological jobs of species in the wild remaining parts a need.

V. Mechanical Advances in Hereditary Exploration

1. **Cutting edge Sequencing**

Cutting edge sequencing innovations have reformed hereditary examination by empowering the quick and savvy investigation of whole genomes. This has essentially extended how we might interpret the hereditary variety inside and between populaces.

1. **Advantages of Cutting edge Sequencing**

High Throughput: Sequencing enormous volumes of hereditary material in a brief time frame.

Cost-Viability: Decreased costs contrasted with conventional sequencing techniques.

More profound Experiences: Giving itemized data on hereditary variety, design, and capability.

B. CRISPR Innovation

The Bunched Consistently Interspaced Short Palindromic Rehashes (CRISPR) innovation offers extraordinary accuracy in hereditary control. While its utilization in untamed life preservation is profoundly discussed, it holds the potential for resolving explicit hereditary issues in hostage populaces.

1. **Quality Altering for Infection Obstruction**

CRISPR innovation could be utilized to alter qualities related with sickness helplessness, making populaces with improved protection from dangers like arising irresistible illnesses.

C. Resident Science and DNA Barcoding

Drawing in resident researchers in hereditary examination has become progressively achievable with the coming of DNA barcoding. This approach permits non-specialists to add to biodiversity observing by gathering and dissecting hereditary examples.

1. **Model: The eBird Task**

The eBird project, which centers around bird observing, consolidates DNA barcoding. Resident researchers can gather feather tests, adding to the comprehension of bird populaces and hereditary variety.

VI. Contextual analyses: Hereditary Exploration in real life

1. **Contextual investigation 1: Florida Puma Preservation**
   Hereditary exploration assumed an essential part in the preservation of the Florida jaguar, a populace that confronted hereditary issues because of a little establishing populace. To address inbreeding despondency, eight female Texas cougars were presented, improving the genetic supply and advancing populace wellbeing.
2. **Contextual investigation 2: Tasmanian Villain Facial Growth Illness**

Hereditary exploration on Tasmanian villains has been instrumental in understanding and fighting the overwhelming facial cancer illness. Recognizing hereditary markers related with illness obstruction is essential for creating preservation systems to safeguard the species.

VII. Future Bearings: Incorporating Hereditary qualities into Protection Practices

1. **Scene Hereditary qualities**
   Scene hereditary qualities investigates the connection between hereditary variety and scene highlights. Coordinating scene hereditary qualities into

preservation arranging recognizes hallways, hindrances, and regions basic for keeping up with hereditary availability.

2. **Versatile Administration Systems**

   As environmental change speeds up, hereditary examination becomes fundamental for figuring out the versatile capability of populaces. Protection methodologies need to integrate hereditary data to assist species with adapting to changing ecological circumstances.

3. **Worldwide Coordinated effort in Hereditary Exploration**

Advancing worldwide cooperation in hereditary exploration upgrades the sharing of hereditary information and assets. Laying out hereditary information bases and organizations cultivates an aggregate way to deal with biodiversity protection.

Chapter 5

Community Involvement And Sustainable Practices

In a period set apart by fast urbanization, mechanical progression, and natural difficulties, the requirement for local area contribution and feasible practices has become fundamental. The interconnectedness of networks and their surroundings requires an aggregate work to guarantee an agreeable and economical future. This exhaustive investigation digs into the meaning of local area inclusion and manageable works on, looking at their singular parts, common impact, and the extraordinary potential they hold for social orders around the world.

1. **Grasping People group Association**
1. **Definition and Extension**
   Local area inclusion alludes to the dynamic commitment of people inside a local area to add to its prosperity and improvement. It incorporates a wide range of exercises, including chipping in, city support, and cooperative critical thinking. The extent of local area association stretches out past topographical limits, exemplifying different gatherings with shared interests, values, or objectives.
2. **Significance of Local area Association**

Social Attachment
Local area association cultivates social union by fortifying the bonds among people. Through shared encounters and aggregate endeavors, networks construct a feeling of having a place and solidarity, making an establishment for a strong and steady friendly texture.

Neighborhood Strengthening
Enabling nearby networks is a vital result of dynamic inclusion. By partaking in dynamic cycles and taking responsibility for drives, people become problem solvers, impacting the direction of their local area's turn of events.

Practical Turn of events

Local area contribution is basic to the quest for practical turn of events. Drawing in local area individuals in arranging and execution guarantees that tasks line up with the requirements and upsides of individuals, advancing long haul maintainability.

II. Supportable Practices: An All encompassing Methodology

1. **Characterizing Feasible Practices**

   Supportable practices incorporate a bunch of standards and activities pointed toward addressing the requirements of the present without compromising the capacity of people in the future to address their own issues. These practices range different spaces, including natural, financial, and social contemplations, and are outfitted towards making a harmony between human exercises and the planet's ability to help them.

2. **Mainstays of Supportability**

   Ecological Maintainability

   Saving regular assets, decreasing carbon impression, and safeguarding biodiversity are focal precepts of ecological manageability. Economical practices in this domain include dependable asset the executives, squander decrease, and the advancement of sustainable power sources.

   Financial Supportability

   Monetary maintainability centers around making frameworks that can persevere over the long haul. This includes cultivating monetary development, advancing fair exchange rehearses, and guaranteeing evenhanded circulation of assets to forestall the minimization of specific gatherings.

   Social Maintainability

   Social maintainability underlines the prosperity of people and networks. It includes advancing social value, inclusivity, and admittance to instruction and medical care. Guaranteeing that advancement helps all fragments of society is fundamental for social maintainability.

3. **Interconnectedness of Local area Contribution and Reasonable Practices**

   Common Support

   Local area contribution and reasonable practices are commonly supporting. Drawn in networks are bound to embrace and execute supportable practices, and, on the other hand, the reception of economical practices frequently prompts expanded local area commitment.

   Grassroots Drives

   Numerous manageable practices rise out of grassroots drives driven by local area association. Nearby people group are in many cases the first to recognize natural difficulties and foster imaginative arrangements that line up with their extraordinary necessities and social settings.

III. Contextual analyses: Representing Achievement

1. **Bhutan's Gross Public Joy**

   Bhutan, a little Himalayan realm, has earned worldwide respect for its special way to deal with improvement, exemplified in the idea of Gross Public Satisfaction (GNH). Bhutan's attention on all encompassing prosperity, social protection, and ecological preservation shows the extraordinary force of local area association in molding feasible practices.

2. **Change Town Development**

   The Change Town development, starting in Totnes, Joined Realm, epitomizes a grassroots way to deal with supportability. This people group drove drive centers around building flexibility by restricting assets, diminishing reliance on non-renewable energy sources, and cultivating a feeling of local area independence.

3. **Curitiba's Practical Metropolitan Preparation**

The city of Curitiba in Brazil has turned into a model for feasible metropolitan preparation through drives that focus on open transportation, green spaces, and waste administration. The outcome of these drives is established in the dynamic association of the local area in molding and supporting maintainable practices.

IV. Difficulties and Open doors

1. **Defeating Obstructions to Local area Inclusion**

   Absence of Mindfulness

   Tending to the absence of mindfulness about local area issues and potential open doors for association is pivotal. Training efforts, studios, and effort projects can assist with overcoming any issues and urge more people to partake in local area undertakings effectively.

   Social Imbalances

   Accomplishing significant local area contribution requires tending to social disparities that might block specific gatherings' capacity to effectively lock in. Making comprehensive spaces and stages for different voices guarantees that everybody has the potential chance to contribute.

   Restricted Assets

   Networks with restricted assets might confront difficulties in executing feasible practices. Cooperative endeavors including state run administrations, NGOs, and organizations can give the fundamental assets and support to defeat these difficulties.

2. **Immediately jumping all over Chances for Cooperative energy**

Innovation as an Empowering agent

Saddling innovation can intensify the effect of local area contribution and economical practices. Computerized stages, virtual entertainment, and information investigation engage networks to interface, share data, and carry out feasible arrangements on a more extensive scale.

Public-Private Organizations

Joint efforts between general society and confidential areas can use the qualities of both to drive economical turn of events. Public-private associations can work with asset sharing, development, and the execution of enormous scope projects that benefit networks.

Instruction and Limit Building

Putting resources into instruction and limit building is a proactive way to deal with supporting a culture of local area inclusion and maintainable practices. By furnishing people with the information and abilities required, networks can all the more likely explore difficulties and add to their own turn of events.

V. Worldwide Ramifications and Future Possibilities

1. **The Job of Global Cooperation**

   Tending to worldwide difficulties requires global joint effort. Nations and networks can gain from one another's triumphs and disappointments, encouraging a worldwide organization of information trade to advance local area contribution and economical practices around the world.

2. **Environmental Change Alleviation and Variation**

   Environmental change represents a huge danger to networks around the world, highlighting the earnestness of embracing economical practices. Moderating the effect of environmental change and adjusting to its belongings require a purposeful exertion including networks, states, and worldwide associations.

3. **Forming What's in store**

What's in store holds gigantic potential for extraordinary change through local area association and maintainable practices. Embracing development, inclusivity, and a promise to the prosperity of the two individuals and the planet can prepare for an agreeable and reasonable future.

5.1Importance of Local Communities in Conservation

Preservation, in the contemporary setting, reaches out past the limits of safeguarded regions and public parks. The dynamic inclusion of nearby networks is progressively perceived as crucial for the outcome of protection endeavors. The many-sided connection among networks and their encompassing biological systems positions local people as stewards of biodiversity and essential accomplices in accomplishing economical, environmentally sound practices. This investigation dives into the multi-layered significance of nearby networks in protection, looking at their jobs, challenges, and the harmonious connection between local area prosperity and ecological safeguarding.

1. **The Inborn Association Among People group and Biological systems**

1. **Authentic Concurrence**
   Nearby people group and biological systems have generally existed together, with native societies encapsulating a significant comprehension of the fragile harmony between human exercises and the regular world. Native information, went down through ages, frequently contains important experiences into feasible asset the board and biological system preservation rehearses.
2. **Reliance on Environment Administrations**
   Networks are intrinsically subject to the administrations gave by biological systems to their endurance and prosperity. Clean water, ripe soil, fertilization of harvests, and a steady environment are among the basic administrations biological systems offer. In that capacity, nearby networks have a personal stake in keeping up with the wellbeing and trustworthiness of their general climate.
3. **Social Importance**

Environments hold social importance for some networks, molding their personality, otherworldliness, and conventional practices. The preservation of regular scenes becomes entwined with safeguarding social legacy, supporting the significance of including neighborhood networks in protection endeavors.

II. Jobs of Neighborhood People group in Preservation

1. **Biodiversity Watchmen**
   Neighborhood people group assume a key part as gatekeepers of biodiversity. Their complicated information on neighborhood verdure, frequently obtained through ages of communication, positions them as priceless assets for recognizing and safeguarding jeopardized species and environments.
2. **Feasible Asset The executives**
   Powerful protection requires practical asset the board. Neighborhood people group, profoundly implanted in their surroundings, are strategically set up to embrace and advance feasible practices in horticulture, fishing, ranger service, and other asset subordinate exercises. This guarantees the life span of regular assets as well as supports the vocations of local area individuals.
3. **Checking and Reconnaissance**
   Nearby people group go about as on-the-ground screens, offering eyes and ears in the battle against criminal operations like poaching, logging, and territory annihilation. Their nearness and information on the landscape make them key accomplices for policing and protection associations.
4. **Protection Instruction and Backing**

Drawing in nearby networks in protection training and backing endeavors is imperative for encouraging a feeling of shared liability. By bringing issues to light about the significance of biodiversity and biological systems, networks can become advocates for maintainable practices and ecological security.

III. Challenges Looked by Neighborhood People group in Protection

1. **Financial Tensions**
   Nearby people group frequently face financial tensions that can drive impractical asset use. Destitution, absence of elective occupations, and financial disparity might urge people to participate in exercises impeding to the climate, for example, overharvesting or unlawful logging.

2. **Restricted Admittance to Assets**
   Discriminatory admittance to assets and dynamic cycles can ruin the capacity of networks to take part in protection effectively. Enabling nearby networks includes resolving issues of land residency, asset possession, and guaranteeing that they have a voice in forming preservation strategies.

3. **Clashes Among Protection and Vocations**
   Preservation measures, while pivotal for safeguarding biodiversity, can now and then conflict with neighborhood jobs. For instance, the foundation of safeguarded regions might confine admittance to conventional hunting or fishing grounds, prompting pressures between protection objectives and the quick necessities of networks.

4. **Absence of Acknowledgment of Native Information**

The rich information held by native networks with respect to feasible practices is frequently underestimated or disregarded. Integrating native information into preservation procedures is fundamental for making all encompassing and socially delicate ways to deal with ecological administration.

IV. Examples of overcoming adversity: Local area Drove Protection Drives

1. **Namibian People group Based Regular Asset The executives**
   Namibia's People group Based Regular Asset The executives (CBNRM) program fills in as an eminent illustration of local area drove protection. By allowing nearby networks privileges to oversee and profit from natural life on mutual grounds, Namibia has effectively incorporated preservation with local area advancement, prompting expanded untamed life populaces and further developed vocations.

2. **Local area Woods The board in Nepal**
   Nepal's people group woods the executives framework enables neighborhood networks to oversee and safeguard close by woodlands. This drive has brought about better woodland wellbeing, expanded biodiversity, and upgraded local area strength, displaying the positive effect of local area contribution in preservation.

3. **Gola Rainforest People group Protection Task**

In Sierra Leone, the Gola Rainforest People group Preservation Venture draws in neighborhood networks in the security of the Gola Rainforest. Through instruction, supportable job projects, and local area watches, the task has added to the conservation of this basic biodiversity area of interest.

V. Amazing open doors for Reinforcing People group Contribution in Preservation

1. **Local area Strengthening and Limit Building**
   Engaging nearby networks includes giving them the devices, information, and assets expected to partake in preservation endeavors effectively. Limit building projects can upgrade local area abilities in economical asset the executives, biodiversity observing, and backing.

2. **Comprehensive Dynamic Cycles**
   Consolidating nearby voices in dynamic cycles is fundamental for making protection strategies that mirror the real factors and yearnings of networks. Participatory methodologies guarantee that the advantages of preservation are impartially conveyed and that potential struggles are tended to proactively.

3. **Supportable Business Choices**
   Tending to the main drivers of impractical asset use requires offering reasonable choices for local area jobs. Feasible farming, eco-the travel industry, and worth added handling of normal items are instances of choices that can uphold both preservation objectives and nearby economies.

4. **Perceiving and Regarding Native Privileges**

Recognizing and regarding the privileges of native networks is basic for compelling preservation. This includes perceiving land residency frameworks, guaranteeing free, earlier, and informed assent, and esteeming the exceptional information and practices of native people groups.

VI. Determination: A Way ahead

The significance of nearby networks in preservation couldn't possibly be more significant. As the watchmen of biodiversity and the stewards of environments, their dynamic contribution isn't just advantageous yet fundamental for the progress of preservation endeavors. Perceiving the inborn association among networks and their surroundings, tending to difficulties, and jumping all over chances for joint effort and strengthening prepare for an agreeable conjunction of people and nature.

The way ahead includes encouraging a change in perspective in preservation draws near, moving towards comprehensive, local area driven techniques that recognize the different requirements and yearnings of neighborhood populaces. Thusly, we protect the rich embroidery of biodiversity as well as add to the making of maintainable, versatile networks that flourish close by the environments they call home. As we explore the intricacies of the 21st 100 years, the job of nearby networks in protection remains as a reference point, directing us towards a future where the safeguarding of nature is indistinguishable from the prosperity of the people who possess it.

5.2 Implementing Sustainable Practices in Tiger Habitats

Tigers, lofty and imperiled, are magnetic images of untamed life as well as cornerstone species pivotal for keeping up with the natural equilibrium of their environments. Nonetheless, the endurance of these notable animals is compromised by different variables, including living space misfortune, poaching, and human-natural life struggle. Executing maintainable practices in tiger territories is basic to guarantee the drawn out endurance of these wonderful enormous felines and the biodiversity they support. This investigation dives into the multi-layered difficulties confronting tiger environments, the significance of manageability in their preservation, and compelling systems for advancing conjunction among tigers and nearby networks.

1. **The Territory of Tiger Environments**
1. **Environment Misfortune and Discontinuity**
   One of the essential dangers to tiger environments is territory misfortune and fracture because of human exercises like agribusiness, framework improvement, and logging. As natural surroundings recoil, the accessible space for tigers to meander, chase, and recreate lessens, prompting expanded clashes and decreased hereditary variety.
2. **Poaching and Unlawful Untamed life Exchange**
   Poaching for their skins, bones, and other body parts stays a critical danger to tiger populaces. The interest for tiger items, driven by conventional medication, extravagance merchandise, and saw superficial points of interest, fills unlawful untamed life exchange networks that further imperil these grand animals.
3. **Human-Natural life Struggle**

As human populaces grow and infringe upon normal living spaces, clashes among people and tigers heighten. Tigers might go after animals, prompting retaliatory killings by neighborhood networks. Such contentions imperil individual tigers as well as add to negative insights and perspectives towards their preservation.

II. Significance of Supportable Practices in Tiger Preservation

1. **Saving Environment Uprightness**
   Supportable practices in tiger living spaces are crucial for saving the honesty of whole environments. Tigers are dominant hunters that assume an essential part in managing prey populaces and keeping up with the equilibrium of their environments. By zeroing in on maintainability, we safeguard tigers as well as the heap species interconnected inside their natural surroundings.

2. **Alleviating Environmental Change Effects**
   Tiger living spaces, frequently incorporating different environments like tropical rainforests and fields, add to environment guideline. Economical practices assist with alleviating environmental change influences by saving carbon sinks, keeping up with biodiversity, and advancing strong biological systems fit for adjusting to natural changes.

3. **Upgrading Network**

Manageable preservation endeavors focus on territory availability. Keeping up with natural life passages and bordering scenes permits tigers to move unreservedly between various regions, advancing quality stream and forestalling the disconnection of populaces. This is vital for hereditary variety and the drawn out practicality of tiger populaces.

III. Procedures for Executing Manageable Practices

1. **Safeguarded Region The board**
   Reinforcing Implementation
   Successful insurance of tiger natural surroundings requires strong policing battle poaching and criminal operations. Expanding the presence of park officers, utilizing innovation like camera traps and robots, and encouraging cooperation with neighborhood networks improve the capacity to uphold protection regulations.

   Local area Contribution
   Drawing in neighborhood networks in the administration of safeguarded regions encourages a feeling of pride and obligation. At the point when networks are associated with dynamic cycles, reasonable practices are bound to be taken on, prompting better protection results.

2. **Reasonable Land Use Arranging**
   Distinguishing and Safeguarding Basic Living spaces
   Planning and distinguishing basic tiger living spaces are fundamental for maintainable land use arranging. Preservation endeavors ought to focus on safeguarding these regions and working with legislatures and nearby partners to limit exercises that could prompt natural surroundings misfortune or corruption.

   Advancing Manageable Farming Practices
   Where farming and tiger environments meet, it is essential to advance economical practices. Agroforestry, natural cultivating, and land-use drafting that limits human-tiger clashes can add to both protection objectives and the jobs of neighborhood networks.

3. **Human-Untamed life Struggle Alleviation**
   Executing Early Admonition Frameworks
   Early admonition frameworks can assist with diminishing human-natural life

clashes by making networks aware of the presence of tigers nearby. Advancements, for example, movement enacted alerts, local area watches, and prepared natural life reaction groups can upgrade wellbeing for the two people and tigers.

Pay Plans

Laying out remuneration plans for domesticated animals misfortunes because of tiger predation gives a monetary impetus to neighborhood networks to coincide calmly with tigers. These plans ease the monetary weight on impacted networks and diminish the probability of retaliatory killings.

4. **Feasible The travel industry Practices**

Eco-The travel industry Drives

When overseen capably, eco-the travel industry can create income for neighborhood networks while limiting adverse consequences on tiger natural surroundings. Directed visits, schooling projects, and adherence to severe moral principles add to maintainable the travel industry rehearses.

Restricting Guest Effect

Managing the quantity of guests, keeping up with trails, and executing rules for natural life seeing assist with limiting the biological impression of the travel industry exercises. This guarantees that the presence of sightseers doesn't upset tigers or their natural surroundings.

IV. **Contextual investigations: Effective Execution of Feasible Practices**

1. **Sundarbans Save Backwoods, Bangladesh**

   The Sundarbans, one of the biggest mangrove woodlands on the planet, is home to the Bengal tiger. Reasonable practices in the Sundarbans Hold Backwoods incorporate local area based protection drives, for example, the foundation of tiger reaction groups, schooling projects, and mangrove natural surroundings rebuilding. These endeavors have added to diminishing human-tiger clashes and advancing conjunction.

2. **Periyar Tiger Hold, India**

   Periyar Tiger Hold in Kerala, India, embodies effective local area contribution in preservation. The arrangement of eco-improvement boards, local area based the travel industry drives, and maintainable gathering programs has engaged nearby networks and diminished their reliance on the save's assets. This has prompted better tiger natural surroundings insurance and decreased cases of human-untamed life struggle.

3. **Russian Far East: Place that is known for the Amur Tiger**

In the Russian Far East, the Amur tiger, otherwise called the Siberian tiger, faces dangers like poaching and living space misfortune. Preservation associations have carried out feasible ranger service rehearses, drew in nearby networks in enemy of poaching endeavors, and upheld ecotourism drives. These methodologies have added to an expansion in Amur tiger populaces and the security of their environments.

V. Challenges in Executing Reasonable Practices

1. **Absence of Assets**

   Numerous tiger environments face difficulties because of inadequate monetary and HR. Restricted subsidizing for preservation endeavors, insufficient staffing, and an absence of innovation frustrate the viable execution of supportable practices.

2. **Worldwide Interest for Tiger Items**

   The constant interest for tiger items in the worldwide market, especially in customary medication and the extravagance merchandise industry, stays a considerable test. Endeavors to battle unlawful natural life exchange require worldwide joint effort, stricter guidelines, and expanded mindfulness about the results of supporting such business sectors.

3. **Political and Financial Elements**

Political flimsiness, defilement, and financial variations in certain locales can obstruct the execution of reasonable practices. Building political will, tending to administration issues, and advancing impartial monetary improvement are fundamental parts of fruitful protection methodologies.

VI. Future Viewpoints and Proposals

1. **Innovation and Advancement**

   Headways in innovation, like satellite following, man-made reasoning, and natural DNA examination, offer uncommon open doors for observing tiger populaces and their environments. Coordinating these advances into preservation procedures improves the accuracy and viability of reasonable practices.

2. **Environmental Change Transformation**

   Environmental change represents a critical danger to tiger territories. Preservation endeavors should consolidate environmental change variation systems, for example, establishing environment strong scenes, safeguarding water sources, and working with relocation hallways that permit tigers to move to cooler regions as temperatures increase.

3. **Fortifying Worldwide Participation**

   The protection of tigers rises above public boundaries. Fortifying worldwide participation, sharing accepted procedures, and resolving worldwide issues like environmental change and unlawful untamed life exchange require cooperative endeavors from states, NGOs, and the global local area.

4. **Public Mindfulness and Instruction**

Raising public mindfulness about the significance of tiger protection is essential for collecting backing and cultivating a feeling of obligation. Instructive projects, media missions, and local area outreach drives can add to changing mentalities and ways of behaving towards tiger protection.

5.3 Eco-Tourism and Its Role in Funding Conservation Efforts

In a period where natural preservation is a worldwide objective, eco-the travel industry has arisen as a feasible and significant method for supporting protection drives. By offering explorers vivid encounters in common habitats, eco-the travel industry adds to neighborhood economies as well as produces subsidizes that can be diverted straightforwardly into the conservation and security of biodiversity. This investigation digs into the idea of eco-the travel industry, its standards, advantages, challenges, and its significant job in subsidizing protection endeavors around the world.

1. **Figuring out Eco-The travel industry**
1. **Definition and Standards**

   Eco-the travel industry, short for natural the travel industry, is a capable travel approach that plans to limit the adverse consequence of the travel industry on the climate while advancing protection, manageability, and local area commitment. Key standards of eco-the travel industry incorporate regard for nature, neighborhood societies, and the advancement of ecological training among vacationers.

2. **Vivid Nature Encounters**

At the core of eco-the travel industry is furnishing sightseers with vivid encounters in common habitats. This can go from natural life safaris and bird watching to directed climbs in perfect scenes. The accentuation is on cultivating a profound association among guests and the normal world, encouraging appreciation and comprehension of the biological systems they investigate.

II. The Advantages of Eco-The travel industry

1. **Monetary Advantages for Neighborhood People group**

   One of the essential benefits of eco-the travel industry is animating nearby economies potential. When overseen capably, eco-the travel industry can make occupations, create pay, and add to local area improvement. Nearby people group frequently become dynamic partners in safeguarding their regular resources as they perceive the financial worth attached to the preservation of biodiversity.

2. **Financing Protection Endeavors**

   Eco-the travel industry fills in as an immediate wellspring of financing for protection drives. Extra charges, directed visit charges, and income from eco-cabins or campgrounds can be dispensed to help preservation projects, including natural surroundings reclamation, against poaching endeavors, and local area based protection programs.

3. **Preservation Through Schooling**

Eco-the travel industry gives a stage to natural training. Guests gain firsthand information about the biological systems they investigate, the significance of biodiversity, and the dangers looked by normal living spaces. This elevated mindfulness can convert into help for preservation endeavors and manageable practices.

III. Challenges in Carrying out Eco-The travel industry

1. **Adjusting Preservation and The travel industry Tensions**
   The fragile harmony between obliging the travel industry and safeguarding the uprightness of normal natural surroundings represents a critical test. Overseeing guest numbers, characterizing conveying limits, and laying out reasonable the travel industry rehearses are basic contemplations to forestall unnecessary weight on biological systems.

2. **Guaranteeing Capable Traveler Conduct**
   Eco-the travel industry depends on capable way of behaving from sightseers. Guaranteeing that guests comply with moral rules, for example, avoiding natural life, abstaining from littering, and limiting their biological impression, is fundamental to forestall adverse consequences on nearby conditions.

3. **Framework Advancement and Over-The travel industry**

Now and again, the advancement of framework to help the travel industry, like streets and facilities, can have unseen side-effects. Over-the travel industry, where famous objections experience unreasonable guest numbers, can prompt living space debasement, expanded contamination, and unsettling influence to natural life.

IV. Contextual analyses: Eco-The travel industry Subsidizing Protection

1. **Galápagos Islands, Ecuador**
   The Galápagos Islands, eminent for their one of a kind biodiversity and commitment to Charles Darwin's hypothesis of development, have executed fruitful eco-the travel industry drives. Guest expenses and severe guidelines on the travel industry exercises store protection programs, obtrusive species destruction, and territory rebuilding endeavors, guaranteeing the drawn out safeguarding of this naturally critical archipelago.

2. **Volcanoes Public Park, Rwanda**
   Rwanda's Volcanoes Public Park, home to jeopardized mountain gorillas, has utilized eco-the travel industry as a foundation of preservation.
   Income created from gorilla traveling licenses is reinvested in enemy of poaching

endeavors, local area advancement activities, and environment security, adding to the effective recuperation of the mountain gorilla populace.

3. **Costa Rica's Rainforest Stores**

Costa Rica has earned worldwide respect for its obligation to preservation through eco-the travel industry. The country's rainforest holds draw in eco-cognizant voyagers, creating income that supports preservation projects, biodiversity research, and reasonable advancement drives. Costa Rica's methodology features how eco-the travel industry can be a main impetus for positive natural results.

V. The Eventual fate of Eco-The travel industry in Preservation

1. **Mechanical Reconciliation**
   The combination of innovation, including computer generated reality encounters and advanced stages, can improve eco-the travel industry's compass and effect. Virtual eco-the travel industry permits people overall to investigate and value regular habitats, cultivating a feeling of association and backing for protection regardless of whether they can't genuinely visit the areas.

2. **Broadening of Eco-The travel industry Contributions**
   Expanding eco-the travel industry contributions past conventional untamed life experiences can widen its allure and effect. Eco-accommodating experience sports, social trades, and maintainable agro-the travel industry drives give elective roads to vacationers to draw in with and support protection endeavors.

3. **Reinforcing People group Inclusion**

Future eco-the travel industry attempts ought to focus on local area inclusion, guaranteeing that nearby populaces are dynamic members and recipients of the business. Local area based the travel industry models, where nearby networks oversee and benefit straightforwardly from eco-the travel industry exercises, can reinforce the connection among protection and local area prosperity.

Chapter 6

Legal Frameworks And Policies

Legitimate systems and arrangements structure the bedrock of cultural administration, giving the design inside which regulations, guidelines, and rules guide the lead of people, associations, and states. The turn of events, execution, and authorization of legitimate systems and arrangements are essential for keeping everything under control, defending individual freedoms, and tending to complex difficulties confronting social orders. This extensive investigation dives into the complex universe of lawful systems and strategies, looking at their jobs, development, challenges, and the effect they have on molding the social, monetary, and political scenes.

1. **The Idea of Legitimate Systems**
1. **Definition and Parts**
   Legitimate systems incorporate the general construction of regulations, guidelines, and rules that oversee a general public. They give the establishment to making, deciphering, and implementing decides that guide individual way of behaving, cultural cooperations, and institutional direct. Parts of legitimate structures incorporate protected regulation, resolutions, guidelines, case regulation, and global settlements, all of which add to the foundation and upkeep of an overall set of laws.
2. **Reason and Goals**

Law and order

At the center of legitimate structures is the standard of law and order. This idea stresses that everybody, including people and government specialists, is dependent upon and responsible under the law. It guarantees that equity is directed genuinely, that lawful cycles are straightforward, and that residents are safeguarded from inconsistent utilization of state power.

Security of Privileges

Lawful structures are intended to defend individual freedoms and freedoms. They articulate the essential opportunities and securities stood to residents, laying out a harmony between the interests of people and the aggregate prosperity of society.

Social Request and Security

Lawful systems add to the foundation of social request and security by characterizing adequate lead and giving components to settling debates.

They act as a system for establishing an anticipated climate where people and foundations can work with certainty.

II. The Development of Overall sets of laws

1. **Verifiable Viewpoint**

   The development of overall sets of laws is well established in the authentic and social setting of social orders. Early legitimate codes, for example, the Code of Ur-Nammu in Mesopotamia and the Code of Hammurabi in old Babylon, established the groundwork for classifying regulations and laying out standards of equity.

2. **Precedent-based Regulation and Common Regulation Customs**

   Overall sets of laws all over the planet frequently fall into two fundamental customs: customary regulation and common regulation. Custom-based regulation, established in the English overall set of laws, depends on legal choices and point of reference to decipher and apply the law. Common regulation frameworks, predominant in mainland Europe and Latin America, depend on far reaching legitimate codes and resolutions.

3. **Global Regulation**

The rise of worldwide regulation mirrors the interconnectedness of countries in the cutting edge period. Settlements, shows, and arrangements between states lay out standards overseeing issues like basic freedoms, ecological insurance, and exchange, adding to a worldwide legitimate structure.

III. Classes of Legitimate Structures

1. **Established Regulation**

   Established regulation structures the most noteworthy lawful system in numerous nations, framing the crucial standards and designs of government. Constitutions characterize the dissemination of abilities, lay out the structure for legitimate administration, and frequently incorporate a bill of privileges safeguarding individual opportunities.

2. **Legal Regulation**

   Legal regulation includes regulations authorized by authoritative bodies, like parliaments or congresses. These regulations cover many issues, including criminal offenses, common matters, and administrative structures for explicit businesses or exercises.

3. **Managerial Regulation**

   Managerial regulation oversees the activities of government organizations and authoritative bodies. It frames the strategies these elements should follow and gives components to residents to challenge authoritative choices through processes like legal audit.

4. **Case Regulation and Customary Regulation**

   Case regulation, otherwise called point of reference, alludes to choices made by courts in individual cases. Customary regulation frameworks depend on point of reference as a wellspring of regulation, with choices in earlier cases impacting resulting decisions and laying out lawful standards.

5. **Worldwide Regulation**

Worldwide regulation administers relations among states and other global entertainers. It includes settlements, shows, standard practices, and the choices of worldwide courts, adding to a structure that tends to worldwide difficulties and advances participation.

IV. Strategy Advancement and Execution

1. **Strategy Definition**

   Arrangements are explicit plans or blueprints created to resolve specific issues or accomplish characterized goals. Strategy detailing includes the ID of issues, the investigation of possible arrangements, and the creating of rules that guide direction and activity.

2. **Partner Contribution**

   Powerful approach improvement frequently requires the contribution of assorted partners, including government offices, non-legislative associations, industry delegates, and general society. Comprehensive policymaking processes upgrade the authenticity of approaches and improve the probability of effective execution.

3. **Strategy Instruments**

   Policymakers utilize different instruments to carry out strategies, including regulation, guidelines, impetuses, and data crusades. The selection of instruments relies upon the idea of the issue being tended to and the ideal results.

4. **Strategy Assessment**

Intermittent assessment of arrangements is fundamental to evaluate their adequacy and make essential changes. Assessment processes include breaking down the effect of strategies, taking into account input from partners, and guaranteeing that the planned objectives are being accomplished.

V. Challenges in Legitimate Systems and Strategy Execution

1. Intricacy and Vagueness

Legitimate structures and approaches frequently wrestle with complex issues that include various partners and clashing interests. The intricacy and equivocalness of specific difficulties make it challenging to form understood, direct arrangements.

2. Authorization and Consistence

Implementing regulations and guaranteeing consistence with strategies can be testing, especially when confronted with asset limitations, defilement, or opposition from impacted parties. Compelling authorization components and motivators for consistence are urgent for effective strategy execution.

3. Quick Mechanical Advances

Mechanical progressions present new difficulties for lawful structures and approaches. Issues like information protection, man-made brainpower, and network safety require lithe and versatile lawful reactions to stay up with quickly advancing advancements.

4. Globalization and Transnational Issues

Globalization has prompted expanded interconnectedness, bringing about transnational issues that cross lines. Environmental change, relocation, and worldwide wrongdoing present difficulties that request facilitated legitimate systems and arrangements at the worldwide level.

VI. Contemporary Issues in Legitimate Systems and Approaches

1. Ecological Manageability

Legitimate systems assume a focal part in tending to natural difficulties, including environmental change, biodiversity misfortune, and contamination. Peaceful accords, public guidelines, and neighborhood approaches shape endeavors to advance manageable practices and safeguard environments.

2. Basic freedoms and Civil rights

Lawful systems are urgent for safeguarding basic liberties and advancing civil rights. Approaches tending to segregation, imbalance, and admittance to schooling and medical services add to building comprehensive social orders.

3. Advanced Privileges and Protection

The advanced age has presented new contemplations for lawful structures, especially in the domain of computerized privileges and security. Regulation and arrangements should explore the harmony between mechanical development and safeguarding people's privileges in the advanced space.

4. General Wellbeing Arrangements

The worldwide Coronavirus pandemic has featured the significance of general wellbeing arrangements in answering irresistible illnesses. Legitimate systems play had a basic impact in working with general wellbeing measures, immunization missions, and worldwide collaboration.

VII. Developments in Lawful Systems and Strategy Execution

1. **Legitimate Tech and E-Government**

   The joining of innovation, known as legitimate tech, is changing general sets of laws and policymaking processes. E-government drives utilize computerized stages to upgrade straightforwardness, openness, and productivity in conveying public administrations and carrying out approaches.

2. **Conduct Financial aspects and Bumping**

   Conduct financial aspects standards are progressively being applied to policymaking through the idea of bumping. Approaches intended to impact conduct unpretentiously, without limiting decisions, mean to accomplish positive results in regions like wellbeing, finance, and ecological protection.

3. **Participatory Administration**

   The ascent of participatory administration models includes drawing in residents straightforwardly in dynamic cycles. Stages for public discussion, resident congregations, and cooperative policymaking enable people to add to molding approaches that influence their lives.

4. **Worldwide Joint effort and Multilateralism**

Tending to worldwide difficulties requires expanded joint effort and multilateralism. Global associations, gatherings, and arrangements work with aggregate activity on issues, for example, environmental change, exchange, and general wellbeing.

VIII. Future Viewpoints on Lawful Systems and Arrangements

1. **Environmental Change Relief and Variation**

   As the effects of environmental change heighten, legitimate systems and strategies will assume a critical part in moderating emanations, advancing reasonable practices, and working with transformation measures. Worldwide collaboration will be vital for address this worldwide test really.

2. **Innovative Administration**

   The administration of arising advancements, including man-made consciousness, biotechnology, and quantum registering, will require imaginative lawful systems. Policymakers should explore moral contemplations, security concerns, and the expected cultural effects of these advancements.

3. **Social Value and Consideration**

   Lawful systems and arrangements will keep on developing to resolve issues of social value and consideration. Policymakers should pursue destroying foundational disparities and guaranteeing that general sets of laws add to making just and comprehensive social orders.

4. **Worldwide Wellbeing Security**

The Coronavirus pandemic has highlighted the significance of worldwide wellbeing security. Future lawful structures and arrangements should reinforce global participation, work on early advance notice frameworks, and improve readiness for pandemics and other wellbeing dangers.

IX.Shaping Cultural Administration in a Powerful World

Lawful systems and arrangements are dynamic instruments that shape the administration of social orders, answering developing difficulties and mirroring the upsides of the networks they serve. From the groundworks of established regulation to the complexities of peaceful accords, the intricacy and variety of overall sets of laws highlight their basic job in keeping everything under control, safeguarding freedoms, and resolving squeezing worldwide issues.

As social orders stand up to the intricacies of the 21st 100 years, the continuous advancement of lawful systems and strategies stays fundamental. Advancements in lawful tech, participatory administration, and worldwide joint effort offer promising roads for tending to contemporary difficulties. What's in store requests nimble, versatile, and comprehensive overall sets of laws that encourage equity, maintainability, and the prosperity of people and networks all over the planet. By exploring this complicated scene insightfully and cooperatively, social orders can endeavor towards administration that is impartial, strong, and receptive to the different requirements of their residents.

6.1 International Agreements for Tiger Protection

Tigers, heavenly and imperiled, stand as notable images of the world's biodiversity. Perceiving the critical need to safeguard these glorious huge felines and their living spaces, countries all over the planet have met up to fashion peaceful accords committed to tiger protection.

This investigation digs into the meaning of peaceful accords for tiger assurance, their goals, challenges, examples of overcoming adversity, and the aggregate endeavors pointed toward guaranteeing the endurance of this famous species.

1. **The Worldwide Meaning of Tigers**
1. **Dominant hunters and Biological system Watchmen**
   Tigers, as dominant hunters, assume a urgent part in keeping up with the environmental equilibrium of their natural surroundings. By directing prey populaces, they add to the wellbeing and variety of environments. The deficiency of tigers can upset these fragile equilibriums, prompting flowing consequences for different species and the general working of biological systems.

2. **Social and Monetary Worth**
   Tigers hold social importance in numerous social orders, representing strength, power, and versatility. Moreover, they add to ecotourism, drawing in guests anxious to observe these tricky animals in their normal territories. The financial worth of tiger-related the travel industry can be a strong motivator for protection endeavors.

3. **Preservation Difficulties**

Regardless of their environmental and social significance, tigers face serious dangers, basically determined by natural surroundings misfortune, poaching, and human-untamed life struggle. Thus, tiger populaces have dwindled altogether, with a few subspecies drove to the edge of eradication.

II. The Job of Peaceful accords in Tiger Preservation

1. **The St. Petersburg Statement 2010**
   The desperation of tiger preservation provoked the assembling of the Worldwide Tiger Gathering in St. Petersburg, Russia, in 2010. During this gathering, heads of the tiger-range nations focused on the St. Petersburg Statement, putting forth an objective to twofold the wild tiger populace by 2022, the following Year of the Tiger in the Chinese zodiac.

2. **The Worldwide Tiger Recuperation Program (GTRP)**
   Expanding upon the St. Petersburg Announcement, the Worldwide Tiger Recuperation Program (GTRP) was laid out. The GTRP is a complete, broad procedure pointed toward guaranteeing the suitability of wild tiger populaces. It frames key activities, including environment preservation, hostile to poaching endeavors, and commitment with neighborhood networks, to accomplish the aggressive objective of multiplying tiger numbers.

3. **The Aichi Biodiversity Targets**

The Aichi Biodiversity Targets, took on under the Show on Organic Variety (CBD), incorporate Objective 12, which explicitly addresses the preservation of tigers. It calls for forestalling the eradication of known compromised species and further developing their protection status and recuperation.

III. Peaceful accords and Their Goals

1. **Show on Worldwide Exchange Imperiled Types of Wild Fauna and Greenery (Refers to)**
   Refers to is a urgent peaceful accord pointed toward guaranteeing that global exchange doesn't compromise the endurance of species. Tigers are recorded under Refers to Addendum I, managing the cost of them the most elevated level of security. This posting denies global business exchange tigers and their parts.

2. **Show on Organic Variety (CBD)**
   The CBD is a worldwide deal that tends to the protection of natural variety and the economical utilization of its parts. Inside the CBD system, endeavors are made to incorporate tiger protection into more extensive biodiversity preservation procedures.
3. **The UN Practical Advancement Objectives (SDGs)**

Tiger preservation lines up with a few UN Practical Improvement Objectives, including Objective 15: Life Ashore, which stresses the security, rebuilding, and feasible utilization of earthly environments. Tigers, as cornerstone species, contribute altogether to the wellbeing and strength of these environments.

IV. Challenges in Executing Peaceful accords

1. **Poaching and Unlawful Untamed life Exchange**
   Poaching for tiger body parts, driven by request in customary medication and extravagance merchandise markets, stays a diligent test. The unlawful natural life exchange, frequently worked with by transnational lawbreaker organizations, represents a critical danger to tiger populaces.
2. **Natural surroundings Misfortune and Discontinuity**
   As human populaces grow and infringe upon regular environments, tigers face expanded territory misfortune and fracture. Foundation improvement, agri-business, and logging add to the corruption of tiger natural surroundings, lessening their capacity to meander and chase.
3. **Human-Untamed life Struggle**
   Strains among tigers and neighborhood networks can grow into human-natural life struggle. Tigers might go after domesticated animals, prompting retaliatory killings and negative insights towards these large felines. Moderating these struggles while guaranteeing the wellbeing of the two people and tigers is a complicated test.
4. **Lacking Financing and Assets**

Viable execution of peaceful accords requires satisfactory financing and assets. Numerous tiger-range nations face moves in dispensing adequate assets to protection endeavors, blocking the complete execution of settled upon procedures.

V. Examples of overcoming adversity: Positive Results from Worldwide Joint effort

1. **Bhutan's Preservation Endeavors**
   Bhutan, a tiger-range country, has shown critical outcome in tiger preservation. The public authority's obligation to keeping up with woods cover and executing

hostile to poaching measures has added to a stable and perhaps expanding tiger populace.

2. **Russian Preservation Drives**

   In Russia, preservation endeavors in the Sikhote-Alin Biosphere Hold and other safeguarded regions have added to the recuperation of the Amur tiger, otherwise called the Siberian tiger. Solid enemy of poaching measures and natural surroundings security play played key parts in these triumphs.

3. **Nepal's People group Based Preservation**

Nepal has been commended for its local area based preservation drives. Connecting with neighborhood networks in tiger preservation endeavors, giving motivating forces to protection, and executing hostile to poaching measures have brought about an expansion in the country's tiger populace.

VI. Amazing open doors for Reinforcing Worldwide Cooperation

1. **Limit Building and Innovation Move**

   Limit building, including preparing untamed life implementation staff and giving innovative assets, is fundamental for improving the capacity of tiger-range nations to really battle poaching and screen tiger populaces.

2. **Incorporated Scene The executives**

   Embracing a coordinated scene the board approach includes considering the whole biological system instead of zeroing in exclusively on individual species. This approach is vital for tending to territory misfortune and discontinuity, which are critical dangers to tigers.

3. **Engaging Neighborhood People group**

   Engaging neighborhood networks through maintainable work choices, training, and association in protection endeavors can add to diminishing human-untamed life struggle and acquiring nearby help for tiger preservation.

4. **Fortifying Legitimate Systems**

Improving and implementing lawful systems connected with untamed life preservation, including stricter punishments for poaching and unlawful exchange, can go about as an obstruction and add to the general progress of tiger protection endeavors.

6.2 National Legislation Supporting Conservation

Preservation of biodiversity is a worldwide objective, and countries assume a urgent part in molding the lawful structures that oversee the security of their normal legacy. Public regulation supporting preservation fills in as the spine for endeavors to shield biological systems, natural life, and the general soundness of the planet. This investigation digs into the meaning of public regulation in preservation, analyzing its targets, parts, challenges, and the job it plays in encouraging economical practices to assist present and people in the future.

1. **The Significance of Public Regulation in Preservation**
1. **Characterizing Preservation Targets**
   Public regulation lays out the objectives and goals for protection endeavors inside a country. These goals frequently incorporate the assurance of jeopardized species, protection of basic natural surroundings, economical asset the executives, and the advancement of ecological supportability. Regulation gives a lawful structure to adjusting public needs to worldwide preservation objectives.
2. **Lawful Securities for Biodiversity**
   Public preservation regulations offer lawful securities for biodiversity by assigning explicit regions as safeguarded zones, carrying out guidelines to control human exercises in delicate environments, and endorsing punishments for exercises that compromise natural life or biological systems. This lawful system keeps up with the fragile harmony between human requirements and the safeguarding of regular environments.
3. **Systematizing Preservation Endeavors**

Through regulation, countries lay out establishments answerable for executing and upholding protection measures. This incorporates offices, divisions, or assigned bodies entrusted with checking biodiversity, overseeing safeguarded regions, and directing consistence with natural guidelines. Viable systematization is vital for the outcome of preservation drives.

II. Parts of Public Regulation Supporting Preservation

1. **Safeguarded Regions and Stores**
   Public regulation frequently assigns safeguarded regions and stores to preserve basic natural surroundings and biodiversity areas of interest. These regions might incorporate public parks, natural life asylums, and marine saves, each with explicit guidelines pointed toward protecting the novel biological systems they contain.
2. **Jeopardized Species Security**
   Preservation regulations regularly incorporate arrangements for the security of imperiled and compromised species. These actions might include limitations on hunting, exchange, or living space obliteration that could hurt the populaces of weak species. Moreover, regulation might work with the recuperation and renewed introduction of imperiled species through rearing projects and natural surroundings reclamation.
3. **Feasible Asset The executives**
   Economical asset the board is a vital part of preservation regulation. Regulations might control exercises like logging, fishing, and mining to guarantee that these practices don't prompt the consumption of normal assets or damage

environments. Feasible administration intends to offset human requirements with natural safeguarding.

4. **Natural Effect Evaluation (EIA)**
   Numerous preservation regulations incorporate arrangements for directing Ecological Effect Evaluations (EIAs) prior to undertaking significant ventures. EIAs assess the likely ecological outcomes of proposed advancements and assist with illuminating decision-production to limit adverse consequences on biodiversity.

5. **Contamination Control Measures**

Regulation frequently addresses contamination control to shield biological systems and untamed life from the unfriendly impacts of tainting. This might include guidelines on air and water quality, garbage removal, and risky substance the board, fully intent on protecting natural uprightness.

III. Challenges in Public Regulation Supporting Protection

1. **Authorization and Consistence**
   Powerful requirement of preservation regulations is a perpetual test. Deficient assets, debasement, and an absence of limit can thwart specialists' capacity to uphold guidelines, prompting resistance and exercises that undermine biodiversity.

2. **Discontinuity of Regulations**
   The discontinuity of regulations across various areas can hinder exhaustive protection endeavors. At times, clashing regulation or holes in inclusion might emerge, confusing the coordination required for all encompassing biodiversity protection.

3. **Human-Natural life Struggle**
   Public regulation should address human-natural life struggle, particularly in locales where associations among individuals and untamed life are normal. Adjusting the insurance of species with the necessities and security of neighborhood networks requires nuanced legitimate methodologies.

4. **Environmental Change Transformation**

The legitimate structures supporting preservation should adjust to the difficulties presented by environmental change. This incorporates creating regulations that address moving territories, changing movement designs, and the general effect of environmental change on biodiversity.

IV. Examples of overcoming adversity: Model Preservation Regulation

1. **The U.S. Imperiled Species Act (ESA)**
   The U.S. Imperiled Species Act is a milestone piece of regulation that gives an extensive system to safeguarding and recuperating jeopardized and compromised

species and their environments. The ESA has been instrumental in forestalling the annihilation of various species and working with their recuperation.

2. **The Costa Rican Biodiversity Regulation**
Costa Rica's Biodiversity Regulation is perceived for its inventive way to deal with protection. It lays out a public arrangement of safeguarded regions, advances practical asset the board, and incorporates biodiversity contemplations into land-use arranging and dynamic cycles.

3. **The Untamed life (Security) Demonstration of India**

The Untamed life (Security) Demonstration of India is a vigorous lawful system that means to safeguard natural life and their environments.

It classifies species in view of their preservation status, lays out safeguarded regions, and manages exercises, for example, hunting and exchange to protect biodiversity.

V. Open doors for Reinforcing Preservation Regulation

1. **Incorporating Native Information**
Perceiving and incorporating native information and practices into preservation regulation can improve the viability and social significance of protection endeavors. Cooperative methodologies that include nearby networks and regard conventional biological information add to additional maintainable results.

2. **Improved Global Collaboration**
Given the transboundary idea of biodiversity, countries can fortify preservation regulation through expanded worldwide participation. Sharing prescribed procedures, teaming up on cross-line protection drives, and fitting legitimate structures add to a more bound together worldwide exertion.

3. **Innovation Joining**
The joining of innovation, like satellite checking, DNA investigation, and information driven instruments, can reinforce the implementation and adequacy of preservation regulation. Innovation helps with observing criminal operations, evaluating biological system wellbeing, and illuminating proof based direction.

4. **Public Mindfulness and Schooling**

Regulation can profit from correlative endeavors zeroed in on open mindfulness and training. Connecting with networks in preservation drives, bringing issues to light about the significance of biodiversity, and cultivating a feeling of obligation among residents add to the outcome of legitimate systems.

VI. Future Viewpoints on Preservation Regulation

1. **Tending to Arising Dangers**
As new difficulties arise, protection regulation should advance to address arising dangers. Regulation ought to be sufficiently adaptable to answer issues like

obtrusive species, arising illnesses, and the effects of arising advancements on biodiversity.

2. **Mainstreaming Biodiversity in Different Areas**

   Preservation regulation can be fortified by mainstreaming biodiversity contemplations into different areas, including horticulture, ranger service, and metropolitan preparation. This includes guaranteeing that strategies in these areas line up with protection objectives to make a more coordinated and synergistic methodology.

3. **Financial Impetuses for Protection**

   Investigating financial impetuses for protection inside lawful structures can energize manageable practices. Components, for example, installments for environment administrations, charge motivators for protection agreeable exercises, and green supporting can adjust monetary interests to preservation targets.

4. **Versatile Administration Approaches**

Given the unique idea of environments and the vulnerabilities related with environmental change, versatile administration approaches inside regulation consider adaptability in answering evolving conditions. This includes consistently surveying the viability of protection gauges and changing methodologies as needs be.

6.3 Challenges and Opportunities in Enforcing Conservation Laws

Upholding protection regulations is a basic part of shielding biodiversity and safeguarding biological systems. While preservation regulations lay out the legitimate system for safeguarding normal assets, untamed life, and territories, their adequacy relies upon hearty requirement components. This investigation digs into the difficulties and amazing open doors related with authorizing protection regulations, inspecting the intricacies in question and investigating likely roads for reinforcing implementation endeavors.

1. **Challenges in Implementing Protection Regulations**
1. **Asset Imperatives**

   One of the essential difficulties in implementing protection regulations is the restricted accessibility of assets. Protection organizations frequently face monetary limitations, prompting deficient staffing, hardware, and innovation. Insufficient assets upset the capacity to lead watches, screen untamed life exercises, and answer really to infringement.

2. **Untamed life Dealing and Unlawful Exchange**

   Untamed life dealing and unlawful exchange address huge dangers to biodiversity. The rewarding business sector for extraordinary species, creature parts, and plant items drives criminal operations. Dealers frequently work across borders, taking advantage of administrative holes and making authorization troublesome.

Complex organizations and the high worth put on specific species add to the industrious test of battling unlawful natural life exchange.

3. **Defilement and Absence of Responsibility**

   Defilement inside implementation organizations represents a huge hindrance to compelling preservation endeavors. Pay off, conspiracy, and absence of responsibility can think twice about trustworthiness of authorization activities. Tending to defilement requires fundamental changes, straightforward administration, and the foundation of systems for responsibility inside preservation associations.

4. **Innovative Difficulties**

   Authorizing preservation regulations in the advanced period requires utilizing innovation for observing, reconnaissance, and information examination. Nonetheless, numerous preservation organizations face mechanical difficulties, including restricted admittance to cutting edge devices, deficient preparation, and the fast development of criminal operations that dominate innovative arrangements.

5. **Inadequate Public Mindfulness**

   Viable protection requirement depends on the help and collaboration of general society. Notwithstanding, lacking public mindfulness and training about the significance of biodiversity, preservation regulations, and the results of criminal operations upset the improvement of a proactive local area took part in untamed life security.

6. **Legitimate and Jurisdictional Intricacies**

Protection endeavors frequently include exploring complex lawful structures and jurisdictional difficulties. Various regulations at the neighborhood, public, and world-wide levels might cover or struggle, making uncertainty for requirement offices. Fitting lawful systems and improving worldwide collaboration are crucial for address these intricacies.

II. Potential open doors for Reinforcing Requirement

1. **Improved Worldwide Coordinated effort**

   Criminal operations frequently rise above borders, requiring composed endeavors among countries. Reinforcing worldwide coordinated effort through data sharing, joint activities, and orchestrated lawful principles can work on the viability of preservation authorization.

2. **Mix of Innovation**

   Progressions in innovation offer huge open doors for further developing protection policing. Satellite symbolism, drones, camera traps, and information investigation can improve checking and reconnaissance capacities, making it more straightforward to recognize and answer criminal operations.

3. **Local area Commitment and Strengthening**

   Enabling neighborhood networks and cultivating their commitment to protection endeavors can be an integral asset for implementation. Networks living in vicinity to natural life environments can act as extra eyes and ears, revealing criminal operations and partaking in supportable asset the board drives.

4. **Impetus Based Preservation Projects**

   Motivator based preservation projects can propel people and networks to take part in natural life assurance effectively. These projects might incorporate monetary motivations, local area advancement projects, or different advantages attached to fruitful protection results.

5. **Public Mindfulness Missions**

   Raising public mindfulness about the significance of biodiversity and the outcomes of criminal operations is essential. Very much planned public mindfulness missions can collect help for preservation endeavors, make a feeling of obligation, and add to a culture of untamed life security.

6. **Reinforcing Lawful Structures**

Clear, exhaustive, and enforceable lawful structures are fundamental for successful protection implementation. Customary audits and updates of protection regulations to address arising difficulties, close escape clauses, and line up with worldwide norms add to more grounded implementation instruments.

III. Contextual investigations: Triumphs and Examples Learned

1. **The Preservation Outcome of Nepal**

   Nepal's preservation example of overcoming adversity features the significance of local area commitment. The foundation of local area oversaw preservation regions and a local area based enemy of poaching approach prompted a critical expansion in tiger and rhinoceros populaces. Motivating force based programs, including income sharing systems, added to nearby networks effectively partaking in protection.

2. **Costa Rica's Installments for Biological system Administrations (PES) Program**

   Costa Rica's PES program exhibits the capability of motivating force based protection. The program monetarily repays landowners for safeguarding and reestablishing regular biological systems. By adjusting financial interests to preservation targets, the program has effectively added to reforestation and living space security.

3. **Savvy Innovation in Protection Implementation**

The Spatial Checking and Revealing Device (Brilliant) is a mechanical development utilized in different preservation regions worldwide. This product works with continuous information assortment, examination, and dynamic in watching and observing endeavors. Savvy innovation has improved the productivity of implementation by giving opportune data and enhancing asset designation.

IV. Future Viewpoints on Preservation Policing

1. **Reinforcing Global Legitimate Instruments**
   Proceeded with endeavors to reinforce global legitimate instruments, for example, the Show on Worldwide Exchange Jeopardized Types of Wild Fauna and Verdure (Refers to) and local arrangements, are essential. Powerful global systems give a premise to joint effort, data trade, and fit ways to deal with combatting unlawful untamed life exchange.

2. **Putting resources into Preparing and Limit Building**
   Putting resources into the preparation and limit working of protection authorization faculty is fundamental. Sufficiently prepared and gifted staff are better prepared to deal with the intricacies of implementation, mechanical instruments, and local area commitment.

3. **Utilizing Resident Science**
   Resident science drives, where individuals from people in general effectively add to information assortment and observing, can be an important asset for implementation offices. Utilizing the aggregate endeavors of residents improves reconnaissance capacities and advances a feeling of shared liability regarding protection.

4. **Versatile Administration and Persistent Assessment**
   Versatile administration draws near, combined with persistent assessment, are important for answering advancing difficulties. Ordinary evaluations of preservation techniques, authorization results, and the viability of legitimate systems empower versatile reactions to evolving conditions.

5. **Fortifying Legal Frameworks**

The adequacy of preservation implementation is intently attached to the legal framework's capacity to arraign and punish wrongdoers. Fortifying legal frameworks, guaranteeing convenient preliminaries, and forcing hindrance punishments add to the general outcome of implementation endeavors.

Chapter 7

Economic Considerations And Conservation Financing

In the perplexing dance between monetary turn of events and ecological protection, the idea of preservation supporting arises as a basic extension. As the worldwide local area wrestles with the difficulties of biodiversity misfortune, territory corruption, and environmental change, finding feasible monetary models that help preservation endeavors has become foremost. This exhaustive investigation digs into the nexus of monetary contemplations and preservation funding, taking apart the intricacies, open doors, and inventive techniques that can orchestrate the basic of safeguarding nature with the requests of financial development.

1. **The Monetary Worth of Biodiversity**
1. **Biological system Administrations**
   Biodiversity is the bedrock of biological systems, giving a horde of administrations fundamental for human prosperity. Environment administrations, going from fertilization and water cleaning to environment guideline and infectious prevention, support agribusiness, medical services, and different businesses. The monetary worth of these administrations is immense, shaping the groundwork of human social orders and economies.
2. **Biodiversity and Strength**
   Biodiverse biological systems show higher versatility to ecological shocks and unsettling influences. Normal frameworks with a different exhibit of animal groups are more versatile to changes, whether brought about by environment changeability or anthropogenic tensions. The monetary advantage of strong environments lies in their capacity to keep up with dependability and efficiency over the long haul.
3. **Biodiversity and Financial Areas**

Numerous monetary areas, like agribusiness, fisheries, and drugs, rely straight-forwardly upon biodiversity. Crop variety, for instance, is urgent for keeping up with strong rural frameworks, while marine biodiversity upholds fisheries that are essential for worldwide food security. The hereditary variety of species likewise fills in as a rich hotspot for creating drugs and other modern items.

II. Financial Tensions on Biodiversity

1. Environment Obliteration

Financial exercises, including urbanization, horticulture, and framework advancement, frequently lead to territory obliteration. As regular natural surroundings are changed over for human use, biodiversity endures, with species confronting the danger of elimination. The financial additions from advancement might come at the expense of irreversible harm to biological systems and the administrations they give.

2. Overexploitation of Normal Assets

Overexploitation of regular assets, driven by monetary requests, represents a critical danger to biodiversity. Deforestation, overfishing, and unreasonable mining can drain biological systems, prompting the deficiency of species and the debasement of environments. Impractical asset extraction endangers the drawn out suitability of financial exercises reliant upon these assets.

3. Contamination and Environmental Change

Modern and horticultural exercises add to contamination, influencing air, water, and soil quality. Moreover, the arrival of ozone depleting substances increases environmental change, affecting biodiversity and biological systems. Monetary exercises that add to contamination and environmental change present roundabout dangers to biodiversity and the security of biological systems.

III. Protection Funding Models

1. Customary Preservation Subsidizing

By and large, preservation endeavors have depended on conventional money sources, including government spending plans, altruism, and non-legislative associations (NGOs). Government organizations allot assets for safeguarded regions, untamed life the board, and protection research. Charitable establishments and NGOs assume a critical part by preparing assets for explicit preservation projects.

2. Installments for Biological system Administrations (PES)

Installments for Environment Administrations (PES) address an imaginative way to deal with protection funding. Under this model, people or elements pay for the advantages got from well-working biological systems. This might incorporate installments for watershed insurance, carbon sequestration, or biodiversity protection. PES adjusts monetary impetuses to preservation results, making a market-based component for financing.

3. **Protection Trust Assets**

   Protection trust reserves are laid out to give a supported and free wellspring of funding for preservation. These assets might be enriched through government commitments, magnanimity, or income produced from ecotourism or normal asset use. Preservation trust reserves work fully intent on creating returns that can uphold continuous protection endeavors.

4. **Biodiversity Balancing**

   Biodiversity balancing includes making up for the adverse consequences of improvement on biodiversity by putting resources into preservation somewhere else. Organizations participated in exercises that influence biodiversity, like land advancement, may balance their effect by adding to the protection or rebuilding of same or more prominent biodiversity somewhere else. This approach intends to offset monetary improvement with biodiversity preservation.

5. **Green Bonds**

Green bonds are monetary instruments intended to raise capital for harmless to the ecosystem projects, including preservation drives. Financial backers buy these bonds, and the returns are reserved for projects with positive natural effects. Green bonds give a channel to directing confidential capital into preservation exercises.

IV. Challenges in Preservation Supporting

1. **Valuation of Environment Administrations**

   Doling out monetary worth to environment administrations is a perplexing undertaking. While specific administrations, like fertilization or water de-contamination, have direct financial advantages, others are more difficult to measure. The immaterial and interconnected nature of biological system admin-istrations presents difficulties in precisely esteeming the full range of advantages got from biodiversity.

2. **Value and Civil rights**

   Preservation funding models should wrestle with issues of value and civil rights. At times, preservation drives might dislodge neighborhood networks or cut-off their admittance to normal assets. Finding some kind of harmony between protection objectives and the privileges of native and neighborhood networks is fundamental for encouraging fair and socially preservation endeavors.

3. **Long haul Supportability**

   Guaranteeing the drawn out supportability of protection funding models is a relentless test. Numerous drives depend on outer money sources, and their prosperity is dependent upon proceeded with monetary help. Creating self-supporting models that produce progressing income for preservation stays a urgent objective.

4. **Market-Based Approaches**
While market-based approaches like Installments for Environment Administrations (PES) and biodiversity counterbalancing offer inventive arrangements, they additionally face difficulties. Issues, for example, deciding fair costs for biological system administrations, forestalling "greenwashing," and tending to the potential for unjust circulation of advantages require cautious thought.

5. **Political Will and Strategy Solidness**

The progress of protection funding is intently attached to political will and strategy security. Changes in political authority, changes in strategy needs, or absence of obligation to protection objectives can endanger subsidizing and disturb long haul preservation methodologies. Guaranteeing a steady strategy climate is pivotal for the viability of protection supporting.

V. Potential open doors and Developments

1. **Maintainable The travel industry**
Supportable the travel industry addresses a potential chance to create income for protection while limiting adverse consequences on biodiversity. Safeguarded regions, untamed life stores, and regular scenes can draw in vacationers, giving monetary advantages to nearby networks and financing for protection drives.

2. **Confidential Area Commitment**
Expanding private area commitment in preservation can open new roads for supporting. Associations with organizations, enterprises, and ventures can prompt creative funding models, like corporate sponsorships, influence speculations, or commitments to biodiversity balancing drives.

3. **Innovative Arrangements**
Headways in innovation, including blockchain and remote detecting, can improve straightforwardness, responsibility, and proficiency in preservation supporting. Blockchain innovation can give secure and straightforward exchanges, while remote detecting apparatuses empower more exact checking of biological systems and biodiversity.

4. **Imaginative Funding Instruments**

Investigating imaginative supporting components, for example, obligation for-nature trades, ecological effect securities, and protection finance systems inside monetary business sectors, presents open doors for broadening subsidizing sources. These instruments can use private capital and adjust monetary motivations to preservation results.

VI. Contextual investigations: Fruitful Protection Funding Drives

1. **The Yellowstone to Yukon Preservation Drive**
   The Yellowstone to Yukon Protection Drive is a transboundary preservation exertion traversing the US and Canada. It centers around associating and safeguarding huge scenes to protect biodiversity. The drive has effectively utilized a mix of public and confidential financing, magnanimity, and organizations to help its preservation objectives.
2. **The Obligation for-Nature Trade in Seychelles**
   Seychelles executed an obligation for-nature trade as a team with The Nature Conservancy and the Paris Club of loan bosses. The trade included changing over a piece of Seychelles' public obligation into subsidizing for marine preservation and environment variation projects. This creative methodology paid off the country's obligation trouble while supporting protection endeavors.
3. **Costa Rica's Ecotourism Model**

Costa Rica's ecotourism model has been hailed as an outcome in creating income for protection. The nation's emphasis on feasible the travel industry rehearses, safeguarded regions, and biodiversity protection has drawn in guests looking for nature-based encounters. Income produced from ecotourism adds to the subsidizing of protection drives.

VII. Future Viewpoints on Preservation Supporting

1. **Mainstreaming Preservation into Monetary Approaches**
   The mix of protection into financial arrangements is fundamental for accomplishing maintainability. State run administrations and global organizations can pursue mainstreaming biodiversity contemplations into financial independent direction, guaranteeing that monetary approaches line up with protection objectives.
2. **Worldwide Participation and Subsidizing Instruments**
   Tending to worldwide protection challenges requires expanded worldwide collaboration and the foundation of compelling financing systems.
   Worldwide coordinated efforts, arrangements, and subsidizing stages can give the size of assets expected to handle gives that rise above public boundaries.
3. **Putting resources into Nature-Based Arrangements**
   Perceiving nature-based arrangements as indispensable parts of environmental change moderation and variation endeavors can draw in financing. Putting resources into reforestation, practical land the executives, and other nature-based arrangements lines up with environment objectives and can earn monetary help from environment finance instruments.
4. **Engaging Nearby People group**
   Engaging nearby networks to effectively partake in preservation and advantage from economical asset the board adds to the outcome of protection

funding. Making components that guarantee neighborhood networks get a decent amount of the monetary advantages created by protection drives encourages joint effort and long haul achievement.

7.1 Economic Benefits of Tiger Conservation

Tigers, as notable and jeopardized species, assume an imperative part in keeping up with the strength of environments and safeguarding biodiversity. Past their biological importance, tiger preservation holds enormous financial worth, adding to economical turn of events, the travel industry, and the prosperity of nearby networks. This investigation dives into the diverse monetary advantages of tiger protection, disentangling the interconnected connections between natural life, environments, and human flourishing.

1. **Natural Significance of Tigers**

Prior to diving into the monetary advantages, understanding the natural job of tigers is essential. As dominant hunters, tigers manage prey populaces, forestalling overgrazing and keeping up with the equilibrium of biological systems. Their presence is demonstrative of a solid and strong environment, with flowing impacts on plant and creature species.

1. **Biodiversity Preservation**
   Tigers are umbrella species, meaning their preservation decidedly influences a wide scope of different species inside their territory. By safeguarding tiger environments, a different exhibit of verdure likewise gets backhanded insurance. Moderating tiger scenes adds to the conservation of whole biological systems, cultivating biodiversity at numerous levels.
2. **Trophic Outpouring Impacts**

Tigers impact the way of behaving and conveyance of prey species, prompting what is known as a trophic fountain. By controlling herbivore populaces, tigers in a roundabout way safeguard vegetation, support the variety of vegetation, and keep up with the natural equilibrium of scenes. This trophic fountain reaches out to other natural life species that share a similar living space.

II. Monetary Advantages of Tiger Protection

1. **Ecotourism and Nature-Based The travel industry**
   Tiger preservation is a foundation of ecotourism, drawing in nature fans, untamed life picture takers, and experience searchers from around the world. Safeguarded regions with tiger populaces become key objections for sightseers anxious to observe these superb large felines in their normal territories. Income produced from ecotourism contributes essentially to

neighborhood economies, making position and cultivating practical turn of events.

Work Creation

The ecotourism business prodded by tiger preservation produces work open doors for neighborhood networks. Occupations range from guides and park officers to cordiality and transportation administrations. This upgrades occupations as well as makes a feeling of pride and obligation among neighborhood occupants towards protection endeavors.

Pay Age

The monetary effect of ecotourism reaches out past direct work. Neighborhood organizations, like lodgings, eateries, and trinket shops, benefit from the deluge of travelers. This extra revenue stream reinforces the financial strength of networks encompassing tiger natural surroundings, diminishing reliance on impractical exercises like poaching or logging.

2. **Social and Instructive Worth**

   Saving tigers adds to the social and instructive extravagance of a district. Tigers hold huge representative worth in many societies, addressing strength, power, and biodiversity. Instructive projects and interpretive focuses committed to tigers give significant opportunities for growth to the two local people and travelers, cultivating a more profound comprehension of the significance of protection

3. **Carbon Sequestration and Environment Moderation**

   Tiger territories, frequently thick woodlands, assume a vital part in carbon sequestration. Woodlands go about as carbon sinks, retaining and putting away a lot of carbon dioxide from the air. The protection of these territories through tiger preservation adds to environmental change alleviation endeavors, giving a biological system administration worldwide ramifications.

   III. Examples of overcoming adversity in Tiger Preservation and Financial Advantages

1. **India's Tiger Preservation Achievement**

   India has arisen as an example of overcoming adversity in tiger preservation, with its tiger populace consistently expanding as of late. The country's obligation to preservation endeavors has prompted an ascent in tiger the travel industry, making financial advantages for neighborhood networks. Well known tiger saves like Ranthambhore and Jim Corbett have become flourishing centers for ecotourism, drawing in guests from around the world.

2. **Bhutan's Protection Model**

   Bhutan, another tiger-range country, has carried out a novel preservation model that coordinates tiger insurance with manageable turn of events. The country's obligation to keeping up with woods cover lines up with its Gross Public Bliss reasoning. Tiger protection has turned into a foundation of Bhutan's ecotourism system, adding to both preservation objectives and financial prosperity.

3. **The Russian Far East and Amur Tigers**

In the Russian Far East, purposeful endeavors to safeguard Amur tigers have yielded positive outcomes. Severe enemy of poaching measures and living space protection drives have upheld the recuperation of Amur tiger populaces. This achievement has added to worldwide tiger protection as well as situated the locale as an arising objective for natural life the travel industry.

IV. Difficulties and Contemplations in Tiger Preservation Financial aspects

While the monetary advantages of tiger preservation are significant, challenges endure, requiring cautious thought and versatile techniques.

1. **Human-Untamed life Struggle**

As tiger populaces recuperate, examples of human-untamed life struggle might emerge. Tigers wandering into human-ruled scenes can prompt struggles with nearby networks, particularly those participated in farming or domesticated animals raising.

Offsetting preservation objectives with the requirements and wellbeing of networks is a basic thought.

2. **Framework Improvement**

Quick foundation improvement, while urgent for financial development, can represent a danger to tiger territories. Streets, rail routes, and other advancement ventures might piece scenes, upsetting untamed life passages and expanding the gamble of human-natural life struggle. Guaranteeing manageable advancement rehearses that consider preservation needs is fundamental.

3. **Poaching and Unlawful Untamed life Exchange**

Poaching stays a tenacious danger to tiger populaces, driven by interest for tiger parts in conventional medication and the unlawful natural life exchange. Actually battling poaching requires powerful authorization measures, global coordinated effort, and tending to the underlying drivers driving the interest for tiger items.

4. **Environmental Change**

Environmental change presents difficulties to tiger living spaces, influencing vegetation, prey accessibility, and water sources. Adjusting preservation methodologies to address the effects of environmental change is essential for guaranteeing the drawn out suitability of tiger populaces and the biological systems they occupy.

V. Future Bearings and Valuable open doors in Tiger Preservation Financial aspects

1. **Local area Based Preservation Models**

   Engaging neighborhood networks through local area based protection models can upgrade the monetary advantages of tiger preservation. Including people group in navigation, income sharing systems, and reasonable asset the executives rehearses encourages a feeling of pride and obligation to preservation objectives.

2. **Innovation and Development**

   Progressions in innovation, for example, remote detecting, camera traps, and information examination, offer new open doors for observing tiger populaces and their environments. Coordinating innovation into protection techniques upgrades productivity, empowers better information driven direction, and adds to the progress of against poaching endeavors.

3. **Practical Supporting Systems**

   Investigating practical supporting systems past ecotourism, for example, installments for environment administrations (PES) or imaginative financing models like green bonds, can differentiate income streams for tiger preservation. These components adjust financial motivations to protection results, advancing long haul manageability.

4. **Transboundary Cooperation**

   Tiger environments frequently range various nations, requiring transboundary cooperation for powerful preservation. Local drives, joint watching endeavors, and data sharing systems can upgrade the preservation influence, giving a comprehensive way to deal with tiger insurance and monetary advantages.

   7.2 Funding Models for Sustainable Conservation Efforts

   Manageable protection endeavors are essential in tending to the worldwide difficulties of biodiversity misfortune, natural surroundings debasement, and environmental change. Nonetheless, acknowledging successful protection requires significant monetary assets. This investigation digs into different subsidizing models that help practical preservation drives. From customary ways to deal with inventive instruments, understanding how to back protection endeavors is fundamental for the drawn out soundness of environments and the prosperity of networks reliant upon normal assets.

1. **The Basic of Economical Preservation Financing**

1. **Biodiversity Emergency**
   The planet is presently encountering a biodiversity emergency, with species confronting extraordinary dangers of eradication. Living space misfortune, contamination, environmental change, and overexploitation of regular assets add to the corruption of biological systems. Reasonable preservation endeavors are pivotal to moderate these dangers and protect the sensitive equilibrium of biodiversity.

2. **Biological system Administrations and Human Prosperity**
   Biological systems give a scope of administrations fundamental for human prosperity, including clean air and water, prolific soil, and environment guideline. Protecting biodiversity and solid biological systems isn't just a moral objective yet additionally basic for guaranteeing the versatility of networks that rely upon these administrations.

3. **The Job of Financing in Preservation**

   Powerful preservation requires monetary ventures for exercises, for example, environment security, natural life observing, against poaching endeavors, and local area commitment.

   Distinguishing supportable subsidizing models guarantees the progression of protection drives and works with the improvement of procedures that line up with long haul natural and social objectives.

   II. Conventional Financing Models for Preservation

1. **Government Subsidizing**
   Legislatures assume a focal part in financing preservation endeavors through public spending plans and devoted organizations. Financing upholds the creation and the executives of safeguarded regions, natural life stores, and preservation research. Government-supported protection drives frequently structure the foundation of public biodiversity conservation systems.

2. **Generosity and Non-Administrative Associations (NGOs)**
   Humanitarian associations and NGOs contribute essentially to protection subsidizing. Enriched establishments, magnanimous gifts, and awards support a wide exhibit of undertakings, from species insurance to territory rebuilding. These elements frequently work on a worldwide scale, tending to preservation challenges in different locales.

3. **Worldwide Guide and Awards**

   Global collaboration and help add to protection subsidizing, particularly in areas confronting intense biodiversity dangers. States, intergovernmental associations, and benefactor countries offer monetary help for projects focused on biodiversity conservation, supportable asset the executives, and limit building.

III. Inventive Financing Models for Practical Protection

1. **Installments for Biological system Administrations (PES)**

   Installments for Environment Administrations (PES) address a creative methodology where people or elements pay for the advantages got from well-working biological systems. This can incorporate administrations like carbon sequestration, water decontamination, and biodiversity protection. PES adjusts monetary motivations to ecological results, encouraging supportable protection rehearses.

2. **Preservation Trust Assets**

   Preservation trust reserves are laid out to give maintained and free funding to protection drives. These assets, frequently invested through government commitments, charity, or income created from ecotourism, work fully intent on producing returns that can uphold continuous protection endeavors.

3. **Green Bonds**

   Green bonds are monetary instruments intended to raise capital for harmless to the ecosystem projects, including protection drives. Financial backers buy these bonds, and the returns are reserved for projects with positive ecological effects. Green bonds give a channel to diverting confidential capital into protection exercises.

4. **Obligation for-Nature Trades**

   Obligation for-nature trades include changing over a piece of a country's obligation into financing for preservation or practical improvement projects. These trades, frequently haggled with loan boss countries or foundations, give monetary alleviation while supporting ecological drives.

5. **Influence Ventures**

   Influence ventures include distributing cash-flow to projects that produce both monetary returns and positive social or natural effects. With regards to protection, influence speculations can support feasible endeavors, local area based preservation drives, and ventures with quantifiable preservation results.

IV. Challenges in Practical Protection Financing

1. **Reliance on Momentary Financing**

   Numerous protection endeavors face the test of depending on momentary money sources, which can prompt venture shakiness and vulnerability. Creating maintainable subsidizing models includes changing from project-explicit financing to long haul responsibilities that address progressing preservation needs.

2. **Absence of Financial Valuation of Environment Administrations**
   Doling out financial worth to biological system administrations, like clean air, water, and fertilization, stays a test. The absence of hearty financial valuation can impede the improvement of subsidizing models that actually catch the full scope of advantages got from solid biological systems.

3. **Tending to Underlying drivers**
   Maintainable preservation requires tending to the underlying drivers of biodiversity misfortune, which frequently come from more extensive issues, for example, neediness, impractical asset use, and deficient administration. Creating financing models that address these underlying drivers and cultivate all encompassing arrangements is fundamental for long haul achievement.

4. **Adjusting Preservation and Advancement**

The pressure among preservation and improvement objectives can present difficulties for subsidizing models. Finding some kind of harmony that guarantees financial advancement while saving biodiversity requires nuanced approaches and cautious thought of the social and monetary necessities of networks.

V. Contextual analyses: Triumphs in Maintainable Preservation Subsidizing

1. **Costa Rica's Installments for Environment Administrations (PES) Program**
   Costa Rica's PES program is a prominent outcome in reasonable preservation subsidizing. Sent off in the last part of the 1990s, the program repays landowners for protecting and reestablishing normal environments. By doling out financial worth to administrations, for example, carbon sequestration and water protection, the PES program has turned into a worldwide model for adjusting monetary motivations to preservation objectives.

2. **Namibia's People group Based Regular Asset The executives**
   Namibia's people group based normal asset the executives (CBNRM) approach is a fruitful illustration of manageable preservation financing. Through the foundation of collective conservancies, nearby networks gain responsibility for and the travel industry exercises, producing income through ecotourism and prize hunting. This model adjusts protection objectives to financial impetuses for networks.

3. **The Tropical Backwoods Preservation Act (TFCA)**

The Tropical Backwoods Preservation Act, sanctioned by the US, upholds obligation for-nature trades with accomplice nations. In these arrangements, a part of a country's obligation to the U.S. is pardoned in return for responsibilities to put resources into preservation projects. The TFCA has been instrumental in diverting monetary assets to biodiversity protection endeavors.

VI. Potential open doors and Future Bearings in Supportable Protection Subsidizing

1. **Confidential Area Commitment**
   Expanding private area commitment in reasonable preservation financing presents huge open doors. Associations with organizations, partnerships, and ventures can prompt creative supporting models, corporate social obligation drives, and interests in preservation amicable practices.

2. **Mainstreaming Protection in Monetary Business sectors**
   Mainstreaming protection contemplations in monetary business sectors includes coordinating ecological, social, and administration (ESG) factors into speculation choices. This can draw in a more extensive scope of financial backers to help preservation drives and make monetary instruments that focus on the two returns and positive natural effects.

3. **Mechanical Arrangements**
   Progressions in innovation, including blockchain, satellite observing, and information examination, offer chances to improve straightforwardness, responsibility, and productivity in reasonable protection subsidizing. Utilizing innovation can work on the observing of undertakings, work with secure exchanges, and give constant information to independent direction.

4. **Worldwide Coordinated effort and Financing Stages**

   Tending to worldwide protection challenges requires expanded joint effort and the foundation of powerful financing stages. Global drives, organizations, and facilitated endeavors can pool assets, share information, and offer monetary help for preservation projects that length various nations.

7.3 Public-Private Partnerships in Tiger Protection

Public-private associations in tiger security unite government offices, non-benefit associations, and confidential ventures to altogether address the difficulties confronting tiger preservation. By utilizing assets, mastery, and development from both the general population and confidential areas, these coordinated efforts improve hostile to poaching endeavors, territory safeguarding, and local area commitment. Confidential undertakings might contribute subsidizing, innovation, or strategic help, while legislatures give administrative systems and protection arrangements. This cooperative energy encourages a comprehensive methodology, guaranteeing the drawn out endurance of tigers and their biological systems while adjusting protection objectives to feasible financial turn of events.

Chapter 8

Education And Awareness

Schooling and mindfulness assume essential parts in shaping social orders, encouraging informed direction, and driving positive change. With regards to worldwide difficulties like ecological preservation, civil rights, and supportable turn of events, the meaning of schooling and mindfulness turns out to be much more articulated. This complete investigation digs into the multi-layered parts of instruction and mindfulness, inspecting their effect on people, networks, and the world in general. From formal schooling systems to grassroots mindfulness crusades, the excursion towards an additional cognizant and supportable future is unpredictably woven into the texture of information and edification.

1. **The Force of Schooling: Building Starting points for Economical Social orders**
1. **Formal School Systems**
   Essential and Auxiliary Instruction
   Essential and auxiliary instruction lay the basis for people, furnishing them with primary information and abilities. Coordinating maintainability and ecological schooling into the educational program develops a feeling of obligation towards the planet, cultivating naturally cognizant propensities since the beginning.
   Advanced education
   Advanced education establishments assume a urgent part in forming future pioneers, experts, and change-creators. By consolidating maintainability studies, moral initiative, and interdisciplinary methodologies into advanced education, organizations add to the improvement of an age prepared to address complex worldwide difficulties.
2. **Long lasting Learning**

Instruction isn't bound to formal establishments; it is a deep rooted venture. Empowering persistent learning through grown-up training programs, online courses, and local area studios guarantees that people stay versatile and educated in the face regarding developing difficulties. Long lasting learning supports a culture of interest, decisive reasoning, and development.

II. Natural Schooling: Sustaining Stewards of the Earth

1. **Figuring out Biological systems**
   Ecological schooling engages people with the information on biological systems, biodiversity, and the interconnectedness of every single living thing. By encouraging a comprehension of the sensitive harmony among people and nature, ecological instruction lays the foundation for supportable practices and mindful navigation.

2. **Preservation Mindfulness**
   Instructive drives revolved around preservation make mindfulness about jeopardized species, living space assurance, and the outcomes of human exercises on the climate. Preservation schooling imparts a need to get moving and obligation, persuading people to effectively partake in endeavors to safeguard biodiversity.

3. **Environmental Change Schooling**

Tending to environmental change requires a very much educated people. Environmental change instruction outfits people with the comprehension of environment science, the effects of an Earth-wide temperature boost, and the direness of relief and variation measures. Informed residents are bound to help arrangements and practices that battle environmental change.

III. Civil rights Training: Cultivating Inclusivity and Balance

1. **Variety and Incorporation**
   Schooling assumes an essential part in molding mentalities towards variety and advancing inclusivity. By coordinating different points of view into educational programs and encouraging open conversations, instructive establishments add to the production of lenient and tolerating social orders.

2. **Orientation Equity Instruction**
   Advancing orientation equity through instruction includes testing generalizations, tending to predispositions, and enabling people to challenge biased rehearses. Schooling turns into an impetus for cultural change, separating orientation obstructions and encouraging conditions where everybody has equivalent open doors.

3. **Common freedoms Training**

Common freedoms training ingrains a feeling of equity, balance, and compassion. By showing key expectations, instructive drives add to the making of social orders that regard and safeguard the privileges of each and every person, cultivating a culture of equity and responsibility.

IV. Innovation and Instruction: Connecting Holes and Extending Access

1. **Computerized Education**

   In the computerized age, guaranteeing advanced education is fundamental for evenhanded admittance to data and valuable open doors. Advanced proficiency schooling enables people to explore the computerized scene dependably, basically assess online data, and saddle innovation for positive change.

2. **Web based Learning Stages**

   Web based learning stages have reformed instruction, making information open to a worldwide crowd. From Monstrous Open Web-based Courses (MOOCs) to virtual study halls, online schooling enlarges admittance to quality learning assets, especially for those in remote or underserved networks.

3. **The Job of Virtual Entertainment**

Virtual entertainment stages have become integral assets for schooling and mindfulness. They work with the fast scattering of data, interface similar people and networks, and enhance social and ecological missions. Utilizing virtual entertainment for instructive purposes adds to making educated and connected with worldwide residents.

V. Grassroots Mindfulness Missions: Assembling People group for Change

1. **Local area Based Drives**

   Grassroots mindfulness crusades, started at the local area level, address explicit issues looked by neighborhood populaces. These missions frequently influence local area commitment, social pertinence, and local area pioneers to spread data and activate aggregate activity.

2. **Craftsmanship and Culture for Mindfulness**

   Imaginative articulations, including visual expressions, music, writing, and theater, act as strong mechanisms for passing on messages of mindfulness and social change. Incorporating craftsmanship and culture into instructive drives enamors crowds and encourages close to home associations, making mindfulness more effective and persevering.

3. **Backing and Activism**

Enabling people to become promoters and activists is a center component of grassroots mindfulness crusades. By giving data, apparatuses, and stages for support, these drives prepare networks to take part effectively in friendly, ecological, and political developments.

VI. Challenges in Training and Mindfulness

1. **Access Abberations**

   Differences in admittance to schooling, both inside and between nations, stay a critical test. Restricted admittance to quality training propagates social disparities, impeding the improvement of educated and engaged networks.

2. **Falsehood**

   The multiplication of deception and disinformation represents a danger to the viability of mindfulness crusades. Teaching people to basically assess data sources and advancing media proficiency are critical in fighting the spread of misleading data.

3. **Protection from Change**

Protection from change is a typical test in endeavors to bring issues to light and advance economical practices. Conquering dug in convictions and cultivating an eagerness to embrace new viewpoints and ways of behaving require designated instructive systems and local area commitment.

VII. Examples of overcoming adversity: Extraordinary Effect of Schooling and Mindfulness

1. **The Green Schools Development**

   The Green Schools development centers around changing instructive foundations into reasonable and naturally cognizant elements. By coordinating ecological instruction, asset effectiveness, and manageable practices, Green Schools add to making earth proficient and capable residents.

2. **The Effect of Worldwide Environment Strikes**

   Driven by youth activists, for example, Greta Thunberg, worldwide environment strikes have prepared huge number of people to request heinous act on environmental change. These developments grandstand the groundbreaking force of mindfulness crusades in preparing aggregate activity and impacting strategy choices.

3. **Local area Drove Protection Drives**

Local area drove protection drives, driven by grassroots mindfulness crusades, have effectively saved biodiversity in different districts. These drives enable nearby networks to take responsibility for regular assets and effectively partake in preservation endeavors.

VIII. Amazing open doors and Future Headings

1. **Interdisciplinary Training**

   Advancing interdisciplinary training cultivates an all encompassing comprehension of complicated worldwide difficulties. Incorporating disciplines like ecological science, sociologies, and humanities empowers people to get a handle on the interconnected idea of contemporary issues.

2. **Worldwide Coordinated efforts in Schooling**

   Worldwide joint efforts in training work with the trading of information, assets, and best practices. Worldwide associations set out open doors for shared opportunities for growth, multicultural points of view, and aggregate endeavors in tending to worldwide difficulties.

3. **Mechanical Advancements for Schooling**

   Headways in innovation, including computer generated reality, man-made brainpower, and intuitive learning stages, present chances to upgrade instructive encounters. Incorporating these advancements into schooling can make learning really captivating, open, and powerful.

4. **Developing Decisive Reasoning**

Enabling people with decisive reasoning abilities is fundamental for exploring a quickly impacting world. Schooling ought to focus on the improvement of scientific reasoning, critical thinking, and the capacity to fundamentally assess data.

8.1 Importance of Public Awareness in Conservation

Preservation, the cautious administration and security of normal assets, is a basic part in tending to the ecological difficulties that our planet faces. From environmental change and territory annihilation to the deficiency of biodiversity, the requirement for protection has never been seriously squeezing. One key angle that can't be neglected in the preservation condition is the significance of public mindfulness. Public mindfulness fills in as the establishment for encouraging a feeling of obligation, understanding, and responsibility among people and networks towards economical practices. In this paper, we will dig into the multi-layered meaning of public mindfulness in protection endeavors and investigate how an educated and connected with public can add to building a maintainable future.

Training and Understanding:

Public mindfulness is an integral asset for training. At the point when people are educated about the delicate state regarding our current circumstance, the unavoidable dangers it faces, and the outcomes of inaction, they are better prepared to settle on informed choices. Instruction frames the foundation of preservation endeavors, engaging individuals with the information expected to figure out the complicated harmony between biological systems and the effect of human exercises on them. This understanding is urgent in cultivating a feeling of obligation for the prosperity of the planet.

Conduct Change and Reasonable Practices:

Outfitted with information, people can pursue cognizant decisions in their day to day routines that add to preservation. Public mindfulness missions can feature the ecological impression of ordinary activities, from energy utilization and waste administration to dietary decisions. These missions assume a vital part in empowering social change, advancing eco-accommodating practices, and decreasing the general effect on the climate. Straightforward activities, like diminishing single-use plastics, monitoring water, and picking reasonable items, can on the whole have a huge effect when embraced by a broad, informed public.

Backing and Strategy Impact:

A mindful and drew openly goes about as a strong power in molding popular assessment and impacting policymakers. At the point when a huge section of the populace is learned about preservation issues, they are bound to advocate for strategies that focus on natural security. Public tension can drive state run administrations and organizations to embrace manageable practices, execute severe natural guidelines, and put resources into green advancements. Along these lines, public mindfulness goes about as an impetus for positive change for a bigger scope, establishing a climate where protection turns into a common cultural objective.

Protecting Biodiversity:

Biodiversity is a foundation of a solid and tough environment. Public mindfulness missions can accentuate the significance of protecting biodiversity and the inter-connectedness of every living creature. At the point when individuals comprehend the sensitive harmony between environments and the job every species plays, they are bound to help endeavors to safeguard imperiled species and their territories. Furthermore, mindfulness drives can reveal insight into the effects of exercises like de-forestation, overfishing, and contamination on biodiversity, accumulating support for preservation measures.

Worldwide Cooperation:

The difficulties our current circumstance faces are in many cases worldwide in nature, requiring composed endeavors on a global scale. Public mindfulness encour-ages a feeling of worldwide citizenship and interconnectedness, stressing that natural issues are shared worries that rise above borders. Informed residents are bound to help worldwide joint efforts, arrangements, and drives pointed toward tending to world-wide natural difficulties. Building a worldwide local area that perceives the significance of protection is fundamental for making compelling, economical arrangements.

Emergency Readiness and Strength:

Public mindfulness assumes a urgent part in planning networks for ecological emergencies, for example, cataclysmic events and environmental change influences. Informed people group are better prepared to adjust to evolving conditions, alleviate chances, and answer really to crises. Public mindfulness missions can teach people on environment strength, maintainable agribusiness practices, and measures to safeguard weak biological systems, at last adding to the general flexibility of networks despite natural difficulties.

Associating Nature and Prosperity:

Past the environmental advantages, public mindfulness missions can feature the characteristic association among nature and human prosperity. Concentrates reliably show that investing energy in nature decidedly affects mental and actual wellbeing. By encouraging a more profound appreciation for the normal world, public mindfulness drives add to an aggregate comprehension that the soundness of the climate is complicatedly connected to the wellbeing and prosperity of people. This association can be a strong inspiration for individuals to participate in protection endeavors effectively.

8.2 Educational Programs for Communities and Schools

Instructive projects custom fitted for networks and schools assume a critical part in molding a practical and informed society. As the world wrestles with natural, social, and financial difficulties, the requirement for extensive instructive drives has never been more basic. This paper investigates the meaning of instructive projects, both inside networks and schools, in encouraging mindfulness, engaging people, and adding to the more extensive objective of supportable turn of events.

Local area Based Instructive Projects:

Local area based instructive projects act as impetuses for change at the grassroots level. These drives are intended to draw in and enable people inside nearby networks, tending to explicit difficulties and advancing feasible practices.

Points canvassed in such projects might incorporate natural protection, wellbeing and cleanliness, monetary proficiency, and local area improvement. The vital benefit of local area based training lies in its capacity to fit content to the extraordinary necessities of a specific local area, guaranteeing significance and effect.

These projects frequently include studios, instructional courses, and cooperative ventures that energize dynamic interest. For instance, a local area might take part in feasible farming practices, squander the board drives, or sustainable power projects. By giving functional information and cultivating a feeling of pride, local area based instructive projects add to the improvement of versatile, independent networks equipped for tending to their difficulties.

School-Based Instructive Projects:

Instructive projects inside schools act as the establishment for molding the qualities and viewpoints of people in the future. Integrating feasible advancement subjects into the educational plan furnishes understudies with the information and abilities important to explore an undeniably intricate world. Subjects like natural science, social obligation, and city commitment can be coordinated across different disciplines, guaranteeing an all encompassing way to deal with training.

Additionally, schools can go past customary study hall instructing by consolidating experiential learning amazing open doors. Field outings to biological stores, local area administration undertakings, and associations with nearby ecological associations give understudies certifiable encounters that support the significance of economical living. These projects upgrade scholarly advancing as well as impart a feeling of obligation and compassion in understudies, supporting ecologically cognizant and socially mindful residents.

Building Ecological Proficiency:

Instructive projects for networks and schools are instrumental in building ecological proficiency, which is the comprehension of natural issues, their interconnectedness, and the abilities expected to address them. Ecological proficiency goes past mindfulness; it includes decisive reasoning, critical thinking, and a profound appreciation for the regular world. Local area and school programs that emphasis on natural education make an establishment for informed direction and mindful citizenship.

Ecological education can be woven into different subjects, from science and geology to writing and workmanship. By associating scholarly ideas with genuine models, understudies and local area individuals can get a handle on the pertinence and criticalness of natural issues. This, thusly, cultivates a feeling of stewardship, empowering people to take dynamic jobs in securing and safeguarding the climate.

Advancing Social Value and Inclusivity:

Instructive projects can possibly address social imbalances and advance inclusivity inside networks and schools. By consolidating modules on variety, correspondence, and civil rights, these projects add to the improvement of a socially cognizant and sympathetic culture. Sharpening people to the difficulties looked by minimized gatherings, both locally and worldwide, cultivates a feeling of obligation and empowers promotion for good change.

In schools, programs zeroed in on inclusivity establish conditions where understudies from different foundations feel esteemed and upheld. This upgrades the in general instructive experience as well as gets ready understudies to explore a world described by variety and multiculturalism. In people group, instructive drives can work with discourse and understanding among various gatherings, cultivating social attachment and cooperative critical thinking.

Expertise Advancement for Manageable Living:

Past hypothetical information, instructive projects ought to underscore expertise improvement for maintainable living. This incorporates useful abilities like planting, fertilizing the soil, energy preservation, and waste decrease. By outfitting people with active abilities, these projects enable them to make substantial commitments to supportability in their day to day routines.

Schools can consolidate reasonable activities, for example, making local area cultivates or carrying out energy-saving estimates inside the school premises. Local area put together projects can offer studios with respect to reasonable cultivating rehearses, water preservation, and different abilities applicable to the neighborhood setting. The objective is to overcome any barrier among information and activity, empowering people to execute economical practices inside their homes and networks.

Local area Commitment and Joint effort:

Effective instructive projects cultivate a feeling of local area commitment and coordinated effort. Local area individuals and understudies the same ought to be dynamic members in the growing experience, contributing their bits of knowledge, encounters, and thoughts. This participatory methodology improves the viability of the projects as well as fabricates a feeling of aggregate liability regarding local area and ecological prosperity.

Cooperation reaches out past the prompt local area or school and can include associations with neighborhood organizations, government offices, and non-benefit associations. Connecting with outer partners gives extra assets, ability, and backing for the instructive drives. This cooperative model makes an organization of interconnected elements pursuing shared objectives, enhancing the effect of instructive projects.

Estimating Effect and Ceaseless Improvement:

To guarantee the drawn out progress of instructive projects, it is fundamental to lay out systems for estimating their effect and advancing ceaseless improvement. This includes following changes in information, perspectives, and ways of behaving among members. Reviews, evaluations, and input meetings can give significant experiences into the viability of the projects and regions for improvement.

Ceaseless improvement likewise requires adaptability and flexibility. Instructive projects ought to develop to address arising difficulties, consolidate new data, and stay receptive to the advancing necessities of networks and schools. Customary assessments and partner counsels add to the refinement and manageability of instructive drives over the long run.

8.3 Media and Its Role in Advocating for Tiger Conservation

Tigers, superb and sensational animals, are confronting phenomenal dangers to their reality. As dominant hunters, they assume a pivotal part in keeping up with the equilibrium of biological systems. Notwithstanding, living space misfortune, poaching, and human-natural life struggle have driven numerous tiger species to the edge of termination. In the fight to save these heavenly enormous felines, the media arises as a strong partner. This paper investigates the urgent job of media in pushing for tiger protection, looking at how it can bring issues to light, shape popular assessment, impact strategy, and drive aggregate activity.

Bringing issues to light through Narrating:

Media, in its different structures, has an extraordinary capacity to wind around convincing stories that catch the public's consideration and summon sympathy. By recounting the tales of individual tigers, exhibiting their ways of behaving, battles, and wins, news sources can make a strong profound association between the crowd and these jeopardized creatures. Narratives, articles, and photograph expositions can move watchers into the universe of tigers, cultivating a need to get going and worry for their endurance.

Past customary media, virtual entertainment stages assume a critical part in scattering these stories broadly. Crusades with sincerely thunderous hashtags, charming visuals, and effective narrating can possibly contact different crowds internationally, separating geological obstructions and making a shared perspective about the predicament of tigers.

Forming General Assessment and Mentalities:

Media has the ability to shape popular assessment and impact cultural mentalities towards preservation issues. Through very much created content, the media can feature the biological significance of tigers and highlight the dangers they face.

Positive depictions of fruitful preservation endeavors, for example, renewed introduction projects or local area drove drives, can rouse trust and encourage a conviction that positive change is conceivable.

Negative depictions of unlawful natural life exchange, territory obliteration, and poaching can likewise act as a reminder, convincing the general population to request activity. By outlining tiger preservation as a common obligation, news sources can urge people to rethink their relationship with the climate and backer for strategies that focus on protection.

Pushing for Strategy Change:

Media goes about as a scaffold between the general population and policymakers, impacting the political plan and pushing for strategy changes that help tiger preservation. Analytical news coverage can uncover holes in existing regulation, debasement in natural life exchange, and shortcomings in authorization endeavors. By exposing these issues, news sources can constrain states to make a quick and definitive move to safeguard tigers and their territories.

Article pieces, commentaries, and meetings with specialists can add to informed public talk, cultivating a need to get a move on that policymakers can't disregard. At the point when the media considers legislatures responsible for their responsibilities to tiger protection, it establishes a climate where political will is lined up with the requirement for hearty preservation measures.

Instructive Missions and Resident Science:

Media fills in as an instructive device, giving data that is vital to cultivating a more profound comprehension of tiger preservation issues. Instructive missions, whether through narratives, intuitive sites, or web-based entertainment, can give bits of knowledge into the intricacies of tiger nature, the effect of human exercises, and the significance of saving their environments.

Resident science drives, advanced through media stations, can draw in the public straightforwardly in preservation endeavors. Applications that permit clients to report tiger sightings, partake in territory observing, or add to explore endeavors engage people to become dynamic members in information assortment and preservation drives. By utilizing the aggregate force of residents, media can transform crowds into preservation accomplices.

Featuring Examples of overcoming adversity and Best Practices:

Positive accounts of effective tiger protection endeavors, restoration of stranded fledglings, or local area drove drives can act as encouraging signs. News sources can grandstand these examples of overcoming adversity to show that preservation measures can yield unmistakable outcomes.

This not just elevates the spirits of progressives and networks effectively involved yet additionally moves others to repeat fruitful practices.

Examples of overcoming adversity likewise outline the significance of cooperation between government offices, non-benefit associations, nearby networks, and global accomplices. Media can assume a part in highlighting these cooperative endeavors, stressing the requirement for a diverse way to deal with tiger protection that tends to both natural and social aspects.

Advancing Dependable The travel industry:

The media can add to dependable the travel industry rehearses by bringing issues to light about the effect of unregulated the travel industry on tiger territories and the prosperity of individual tigers. Narratives and articles can reveal insight into cases of abuse, environment aggravation, and exploitative practices related with untamed life the travel industry. By illuminating the general population about the results regarding reckless the travel industry, media can urge explorers to pick moral natural life encounters that focus on preservation and creature government assistance.

Dependable the travel industry stories can likewise feature the monetary advantages of preservation centered the travel industry, exhibiting models where networks have flourished by embracing economical the travel industry rehearses that safeguard tiger territories while giving livelihoods to neighborhood inhabitants.

Challenges and Moral Contemplations:

While media assumes a vital part in upholding for tiger preservation, it isn't without challenges and moral contemplations. Emotionalism, falsehood, and the commodification of natural life for diversion can subvert certified preservation endeavors. News sources should stick to moral announcing principles, staying away from the utilization of poetic exaggeration or symbolism that may sensationalize the situation of tigers.

Moreover, finding some kind of harmony between bringing issues to light and it is fundamental to safeguard the security of tigers. Overexposure to human presence, even through benevolent narratives or photography, can upset regular ways of behaving and add to pressure for these creatures. Mindful media inclusion should focus on the prosperity of tigers over melodrama.

Global Coordinated effort and Systems administration:

Media, with its worldwide reach, assumes an essential part in working with global coordinated effort and systems administration for tiger preservation. Inclusion of transboundary preservation drives, joint examination undertakings, and organizations between nations highlights the interconnected idea of protection endeavors.

By exhibiting instances of effective cooperation, media can move countries to cooperate to address the common test of saving the world's tigers.

Besides, worldwide media inclusion can cause to notice the worldwide ramifications of tiger protection, stressing that the destiny of these sublime animals is interlaced with the strength of the planet in general. This interconnected story can prepare support from different crowds and empower aggregate activity on a worldwide scale.

Chapter 9

Challenges And Future Outlook

The world is described by an unpredictable embroidered artwork of interconnected difficulties, going from natural emergencies and financial abberations to mechanical situations and general wellbeing crises. Understanding the intricacy of these difficulties is fundamental for creating viable procedures that prepare for a feasible and impartial future. This exposition will dig into the diverse difficulties that humankind faces today, investigating the complexities of each issue and inspecting likely pathways towards a more hopeful future.

Ecological Difficulties

1.1 Environmental Change:

Environmental change remains as one of the most squeezing difficulties defying the world. The climb in worldwide temperatures, outrageous climate occasions, and dissolving ice covers are obvious signs of the direness to resolve this issue. Human exercises, especially the consuming of petroleum products and deforestation, add to the collection of ozone harming substances in the environment. Relieving environmental change requires a planned worldwide work to lessen discharges, progress to sustainable power sources, and adjust to the evolving environment.

1.2 Biodiversity Misfortune:

The deficiency of biodiversity, driven by environment obliteration, contamination, and environmental change, represents a danger to biological systems and human prosperity. The elimination of species upsets biological equilibrium, affecting food security, water assets, and medication. Preservation endeavors should zero in on saving living spaces, fighting unlawful untamed life exchange, and elevating manageable practices to safeguard biodiversity.

1.3 Asset Exhaustion:

The impractical utilization of normal assets, including water, soil, and minerals, prompts consumption and natural debasement. Overconsumption and wasteful asset the board add to shortage, worsening social and financial incongruities. Supportable asset the board rehearses, round economy models, and mechanical developments are pivotal for tending to this test.

Financial Difficulties

2.1 Imbalance and Destitution:

Financial variations continue universally, with a huge part of the total populace living in destitution. Pay imbalance, absence of admittance to instruction and medical care, and oppressive practices add to the propagation of destitution. Resolving these issues requires far reaching social strategies, comprehensive monetary development, and endeavors to take out fundamental boundaries.

2.2 Instruction Abberations:

Variations in admittance to quality training upset social portability and add to the pattern of destitution. Difficulties, for example, absence of framework, orientation based segregation, and insufficient instructive assets should be tended to. Interest in schooling, especially in minimized networks, is critical for cultivating evenhanded open doors and economical turn of events.

2.3 Worldwide Wellbeing Emergencies:

The development of worldwide wellbeing emergencies, exemplified by the Coronavirus pandemic, features the weaknesses of medical services frameworks around the world. Admittance to medical services, immunization dissemination, and pandemic readiness are basic contemplations. Reinforcing medical services foundation, putting resources into innovative work, and cultivating worldwide participation are fundamental for tending to future wellbeing challenges.

Mechanical Difficulties

3.1 Online protection Dangers:

The quick headway of innovation carries with it new difficulties, especially in the domain of network safety. As social orders become more interconnected, the gamble of digital assaults on basic foundation, individual information, and public safety increments. Creating vigorous network protection measures, worldwide participation, and moral rules for innovation use are basic to relieve these dangers.

3.2 Computerization and Occupation Relocation:

The ascent of mechanization and man-made consciousness can possibly change enterprises and upgrade productivity. Be that as it may, it additionally presents difficulties connected with work removal, as specific undertakings become computerized. Setting up the labor force for the computerized age, retraining projects, and strategies that guarantee a simply progress are important to address the financial effects of computerization.

3.3 Moral Situations in Biotechnology:

Propels in biotechnology present moral difficulties, from hereditary designing to the utilization of computerized reasoning in medical care. Finding some kind of harmony between mechanical advancement and moral contemplations is pivotal.

Vigorous administrative systems, public talk on moral rules, and interdisciplinary coordinated effort are fundamental to explore the moral scene of biotechnology.

Public Strategy and Administration Difficulties

4.1 Political Precariousness and Struggle:

Political shakiness and struggle upset social orders, prompting compassionate emergencies and blocking supportable turn of events. Underlying drivers, including political defilement, ethnic pressures, and monetary incongruities, should be addressed to advance soundness. Tact, compromise systems, and comprehensive administration structures are fundamental parts of encouraging worldwide harmony.

4.2 Movement and Removal:

Constrained movement, driven by struggle, environmental change, and monetary incongruities, is a developing test. The situation of evacuees and inside dislodged people requires global collaboration, compassionate help, and long haul arrangements tending to the main drivers of relocation. Extensive movement strategies that focus on basic liberties are significant for dealing with this test.

4.3 Worldwide Administration Holes:

The intricacy of worldwide difficulties frequently surpasses the limit of existing administration structures. Holes in worldwide administration, like the lopsided appropriation of force in global associations, impede powerful participation. Reinforcing worldwide administration, improving global foundations, and encouraging multilateralism are fundamental for resolving issues that rise above public lines.

Social and Social Difficulties

5.1 Social Safeguarding:

Social variety faces dangers from globalization, homogenization, and the disintegration of conventional practices. Safeguarding and celebrating social legacy is fundamental for keeping up with cultural lavishness. Schooling, social trade projects, and approaches that shield native information add to the protection of social variety.

5.2 Common freedoms Infringement:

Common liberties infringement persevere all around the world, going from segregation and viciousness to concealment of free discourse.

Maintaining common liberties requires global responsibility instruments, support, and endeavors to address fundamental treacheries. Common society commitment and conciliatory tension assume urgent parts in fighting denials of basic liberties.

5.3 Virtual Entertainment and Falsehood:

The appearance of web-based entertainment has changed correspondence yet additionally worked with the spread of falsehood, counterfeit news, and online can't stand discourse. Tending to these difficulties includes media education programs, truth really taking a look at drives, and dependable web based entertainment rehearses. Offsetting opportunity of articulation with the need to check hurtful substance is urgent for a sound data biological system.

Future Standpoint and Systems for Tending to Difficulties

6.1 Interconnected Arrangements:

Numerous worldwide difficulties are interconnected, requiring all encompassing and incorporated arrangements. Approaches that perceive the relationship of natural, financial, and mechanical difficulties are bound to be compelling. Cross-sectoral joint effort, interdisciplinary exploration, and extensive approaches are fundamental for resolving complex issues.

6.2 Development and Innovation as Empowering agents:

Development and innovation can act as empowering agents for tending to worldwide difficulties. From supportable energy arrangements and accuracy farming to headways in medical care, innovation can assume an extraordinary part. Notwithstanding, moral contemplations, availability, and mindful development should be focused on to guarantee that mechanical progressions benefit all of humankind.

6.3 Global Participation and Multilateralism:

Worldwide difficulties require global participation and reinforced multilateralism. Strategy, cooperative exploration drives, and the pooling of assets are fundamental for tending to difficulties that rise above public limits. Reinforcing worldwide foundations and cultivating a feeling of shared liability are key parts of compelling worldwide administration.

6.4 Enabling Nearby People group:

Answers for worldwide difficulties should focus on the strengthening of neighborhood networks. Drawing in networks in dynamic cycles, regarding native information, and advancing economical practices at the grassroots level add to successful and supportable arrangements. Nearby strengthening guarantees that intercessions are logically significant and comprehensive.

6.5 Training as an Impetus for Change:

Schooling arises as an impetus for tending to worldwide difficulties. Outfitting people with information, decisive reasoning abilities, and a worldwide viewpoint encourages informed citizenship. Instructive projects that underscore supportability, inclusivity, and moral contemplations add to molding an age equipped for handling complex issues.

9.1Ongoing Threats to Tiger Populations

Tigers, magnificent and strong enormous felines, are confronting an extraordinary danger to their endurance. Notwithstanding protection endeavors in late many years, various moves keep on endangering tiger populaces around the world. This exposition will give an exhaustive examination of the continuous dangers to tiger populaces, looking at the perplexing transaction of variables, for example, environment misfortune, poaching, human-natural life struggle, and the effect of environmental change. Moreover, we will investigate the developing scene of tiger protection endeavors, featuring the significance of worldwide cooperation and inventive procedures to guarantee the drawn out endurance of these notable species.

Natural surroundings Misfortune and Fracture:

One of the essential dangers to tiger populaces is the misfortune and fracture of their normal living spaces. Fast urbanization, agrarian extension, and framework advancement infringe upon customary tiger regions, prompting the discontinuity of once coterminous scenes. Subsequently, tigers are separated in more modest pockets of environment, making it hard for them to track down mates and support hereditarily different populaces.

Preservation endeavors should address territory security and reclamation, accentuating the significance of keeping up with huge, interconnected scenes. Drives, for example, the production of natural life hallways and safeguarded regions assume an essential part in moderating the effect of environment misfortune and discontinuity.

Poaching and Unlawful Untamed life Exchange:

Poaching stays a grave danger to tiger populaces, driven by the interest for tiger parts in customary medication, extravagance merchandise, and as superficial points of interest. In spite of worldwide prohibitions on the exchange of tiger items, unlawful business sectors continue, driven by worthwhile monetary motivating forces. Tigers are focused on for their skins, bones, and other body parts, driving numerous sub-species to the edge of elimination.

Reinforcing against poaching endeavors, improving policing, executing severe punishments for natural life wrongdoing are fundamental parts of battling this continuous danger.

Cooperative worldwide endeavors are significant to disturbing unlawful natural life exchange organizations and destroying the monetary motivators that drive poaching.

Human-Natural life Struggle:

As human populaces extend and infringe further into tiger natural surroundings, occurrences of human-untamed life struggle raise. Tigers might go after domesticated animals, prompting retaliatory killings by neighborhood networks looking to safe-guard their livelihoods. Such struggles bring about the deficiency of both human and tiger lives and add to negative view of tigers among impacted networks.

Executing procedures for conjunction, for example, local area based preservation drives, secure animals the board rehearses, and early-cautioning frameworks, is crucial. These actions can assist with moderating struggles and cultivate a feeling of divided liability regarding tiger protection between neighborhood networks.

Environmental Change and Adjusted Territories:

Environmental change represents a complex danger to tiger populaces. Climbing temperatures, changing precipitation examples, and outrageous climate occasions can modify environments and disturb biological systems. These progressions influence the accessibility of prey species and water sources, compelling tigers to adjust to new circumstances. Also, environmental change adds to the increase of existing dangers, like fierce blazes and the spread of illnesses.

Environment versatile protection systems, territory rebuilding activities, and mea-sures to address the effects of environmental change on prey species are basic.

Traditionalists should likewise consider the expected requirement for helped movement of tigers to reasonable territories as environment conditions develop

Absence of Hereditary Variety:

The little and divided populaces of some tiger subspecies add to a disturbing absence of hereditary variety. Inbreeding despondency can bring about diminished conceptive wellness, lower whelp endurance rates, and expanded weakness to illnesses. Keeping up with hereditary variety is urgent for the drawn out wellbeing and flexibility of tiger populaces.

Protection endeavors ought to focus on the foundation and upkeep of hereditarily different populaces through essential rearing projects, movements, and the formation of hallways that work with quality stream between detached populaces.

Lacking Protection Strategies and Authorization:

Notwithstanding expanded attention to the dangers confronting tigers, the execution and requirement of preservation strategies stay lacking in certain districts.

Lacking assets, debasement, and contending interests frequently obstruct the adequacy of preservation measures. Moreover, political unsteadiness in specific regions ruins the foundation and implementation of defensive arrangements.

Reinforcing political will, designating sufficient assets, and upgrading global collaboration are fundamental for tending to strategy holes and working on the requirement of protection measures. Drawing in neighborhood networks in approach advancement and requirement cycles can likewise add to more viable and economical preservation endeavors.

Impractical The travel industry Practices:

While ecotourism can be an incredible asset for protection, ineffectively oversaw the travel industry can represent a danger to tiger populaces. Unregulated the travel industry might prompt natural surroundings unsettling influence, expanded weight on tigers, and the potential for sickness transmission among people and untamed life. Besides, the strain to take care of vacationer request might think twice about needs.

Maintainable the travel industry works on, including dependable guest the board, territory well disposed foundation advancement, and local area commitment, are critical for adjusting the financial advantages of the travel industry with the preservation needs of tiger populaces.

Arising Dangers from Foundation Advancement:

Enormous scope framework projects, like streets, dams, and mining activities, represent an arising danger to tiger territories. These undertakings can prompt natural surroundings obliteration, expanded human-untamed life struggle, and the discontinuity of imperative scenes. The combined effect of numerous foundation advancements compounds the difficulties looked by tiger populaces.

Integrating natural effect evaluations into foundation arranging, supporting for feasible advancement rehearses, and advancing green framework drives are fundamental stages in alleviating the dangers presented by enormous scope improvement projects.

Preservation Endeavors and Developments:

Notwithstanding the overwhelming difficulties, there are empowering indications of progress in tiger protection. States, non-legislative associations, and nearby networks are carrying out imaginative procedures to safeguard and reestablish tiger environments, address poaching, and take part in local area driven preservation drives.

Worldwide Tiger Recuperation Program:

The Worldwide Tiger Recuperation Program, sent off in 2010, is a cooperative drive including tiger-range nations, global associations, and protection partners.

The program means to twofold the wild tiger populace by 2022, the following Chinese Year of the Tiger. It centers around further developing tiger living spaces, reinforcing against poaching measures, and connecting with neighborhood networks in preservation endeavors.

Following the advancement of the Worldwide Tiger Recuperation Program gives significant bits of knowledge into the viability of global collaboration and the difficulties that continue accomplishing tiger preservation objectives.

Brilliant Innovation for Hostile to Poaching Endeavors:

The utilization of Spatial Checking and Revealing Device (Savvy) innovation has reformed enemy of poaching endeavors. This instrument utilizes a blend of GPS, camera traps, and other observing gadgets to follow and break down the development of tigers and likely poachers. Shrewd innovation improves the proficiency of watches, considers ongoing information examination, and adds to the advancement of designated preservation systems.

Coordinating Shrewd innovation into more extensive preservation endeavors assists traditionalists with adjusting their systems in light of ongoing information, working on the possibilities foiling criminal operations and safeguarding tiger populaces.

Local area Based Protection Projects:

Local area based protection programs perceive the necessary job of nearby networks in tiger preservation. Drawing in networks in dynamic cycles, giving elective occupations, and encouraging a feeling of pride over protection drives add to fruitful results. Ventures, for example, local area based ecotourism, reasonable asset the executives, and participatory preservation arranging enable neighborhood inhabitants to become advocates for tiger security.

The progress of local area based protection programs features the significance of considering the requirements and viewpoints of nearby networks while planning and carrying out preservation systems.

Hereditary Administration and Rearing Projects:

Hereditary administration and reproducing programs are fundamental for keeping up with solid and hereditarily assorted tiger populaces. Zoos and preservation associations team up on essential reproducing drives that mean to save hereditary variety, forestall inbreeding, and add to the drawn out endurance of the species. The

Relationship of Zoos and Aquariums (AZA) Tiger Species Endurance Plan (SSP) is an illustration of such cooperative endeavors.

These projects assume a crucial part in supporting the protection of tigers, especially for subspecies confronting huge difficulties in nature.

Transboundary Preservation Drives:

Tigers don't stick to public lines, and viable protection requires transboundary drives that rise above international limits. Undertakings, for example, the Terai Circular segment Scene in Nepal and India and the Core of Borneo drive including Malaysia, Indonesia, and Brunei center around making interconnected natural surroundings that permit tigers to wander uninhibitedly across borders.

Transboundary preservation endeavors accentuate the significance of global collaboration and the requirement for shared liability in protecting the world's tiger populaces.

Innovation Driven Preservation Mindfulness:

Using innovation for preservation mindfulness is a developing pattern in drawing in general society. Computer generated reality encounters, expanded reality applications, and intuitive web-based stages permit people to associate with tigers and their territories in vivid ways. These innovations bring issues to light as well as cultivate a feeling of sympathy and obligation to tiger preservation.

Utilizing innovation in preservation mindfulness endeavors helps contact a more extensive crowd and create support for tiger security.

Installment for Biological system Administrations (PES) Projects:

Installment for Biological system Administrations (PES) programs offer monetary impetuses to nearby networks for keeping up with solid environments and safeguarding biodiversity. With regards to tiger preservation, PES drives can compensate networks for shielding tiger natural surroundings, avoiding criminal operations, and effectively taking part in protection endeavors.

PES programs adjust financial motivating forces to preservation objectives, advancing an amicable concurrence between human networks and tiger populaces.

9.2 Anticipated Challenges in Global Conservation Efforts

Worldwide preservation endeavors are at a basic point, as the world wrestles with a horde of difficulties that compromise biodiversity, biological systems, and the fragile equilibrium of our planet. While critical steps have been made in bringing issues to light and executing protection drives, the street ahead is full of expected difficulties. This paper investigates the multi-layered deterrents that worldwide protection endeavors are probably going to confront, inspecting issues going from environmental change and living space corruption to financial elements and international strains. By understanding these difficulties, we can make progress toward creating strong and versatile techniques that will shape the eventual fate of preservation on a worldwide scale.

Environmental Change:

1.1 Effect on Territories and Species:

Environmental change represents a considerable danger to biodiversity by modifying biological systems and disturbing the circulation of species. Climbing temperatures, changing precipitation examples, and outrageous climate occasions add to living space misfortune, debasement, and discontinuity. Species that can't adjust rapidly enough might confront elimination, prompting a flowing impact on whole environments.

The expected test lies in creating preservation methodologies that are receptive to dynamic environment designs. This includes distinguishing environment strong living spaces, helping species in movement, and carrying out versatile administration rehearses. Progressives should explore the vulnerability of what environmental change will mean for explicit districts and designer mediations likewise.

1.2 Changing Phenology and Relocation Examples:

Environmental change impacts the planning of natural occasions, like blossoming, relocation, and reproducing, disturbing laid out biological rhythms. For transitory species, adjusted environment conditions might influence the accessibility of reasonable territories along relocation courses, prompting befuddles between asset accessibility and the planning of movement.

Preservation endeavors need to represent these progressions in phenology and relocation designs. This requires checking shifts in the way of behaving of species, grasping the biological ramifications, and carrying out measures to safeguard basic visit locales and favorable places along movement courses.

1.3 Sea Fermentation and Coral Fading:

Sea fermentation, basically determined by expanded carbon dioxide retention, represents a huge danger to marine biological systems. Coral reefs, fundamental for biodiversity and fisheries, are especially powerless against the joined impacts of sea fermentation and climbing ocean temperatures, bringing about coral dying occasions.

Preservation techniques should address the mind boggling interchange between environmental change and marine biological systems. This includes executing measures to diminish fossil fuel byproducts, upgrading marine safeguarded regions, and creating imaginative ways to deal with coral reclamation and flexibility.

Living space Debasement and Misfortune:

2.1 Deforestation and Land Use Change:

Deforestation and land use change stay basic difficulties, particularly in tropical districts with high biodiversity. Farming, logging, and framework advancement add to the deficiency of essential woodlands, prompting environment discontinuity and debasement.

The change of regular living spaces into agrarian scenes additionally escalates the human-natural life struggle.

Protection endeavors should defy the financial drivers behind deforestation, advance manageable land-use practices, and backing drives that offset human necessities with environmental conservation. Connecting with nearby networks in economical asset the executives and reforestation projects is fundamental for relieving territory debasement.

2.2 Urbanization and Framework Advancement:

Quick urbanization and huge scope foundation projects further compound natural surroundings misfortune and fracture. Metropolitan development frequently prompts the change of regular natural surroundings into substantial scenes, secluding species and upsetting biological cycles. Foundation improvement, like streets and dams, can section environments and increment openness to already distant regions, prompting expanded poaching and unlawful logging.

Adjusting the requests of advancement with protection requires cautious preparation and adherence to feasible practices. Executing green foundation, safeguarding natural life hallways, and directing intensive ecological effect appraisals are vital parts of exploring the difficulties presented by urbanization and framework advancement.

Overexploitation and Unlawful Untamed life Exchange:

3.1 Poaching and Dealing:

The unlawful untamed life exchange stays a tireless test that undermines various species internationally. Poaching for bushmeat, customary medication, and the outlandish pet exchange represents a huge gamble to many imperiled species, including famous warm blooded creatures, reptiles, and birds. Coordinated criminal organizations frequently drive these exercises, taking advantage of administrative holes and shortcomings in policing.

Tending to unlawful natural life exchange requires an incorporated methodology including stricter policing, cooperation, and local area commitment. Reinforcing punishments for natural life wrongdoing, destroying dealing organizations, and bringing issues to light about the outcomes of buying unlawful untamed life items are fundamental procedures.

3.2 Overfishing and Consumption of Marine Assets:

Overfishing, energized by expanding interest for fish and the utilization of unreasonable fishing rehearses, compromises marine environments. The consumption of fish stocks upsets food networks, influences occupations, and compromises the flexibility of marine conditions. Moreover, horrendous fishing techniques, like base fishing, add to territory annihilation.

Feasible fisheries the executives, the foundation of marine safeguarded regions, and the advancement of dependable customer decisions are basic for tending to the difficulties of overfishing. Coordinated effort between legislatures, fishing ventures, and protection associations is fundamental for carrying out successful preservation measures.

Financial Variables:

4.1 Populace Development and Asset Requests:

Quick populace development puts expanded strain on regular assets, prompting natural surroundings annihilation, overconsumption, and escalated rivalry for land

and water. As human populaces extend, particularly in biodiversity-rich locales, the difficulties of rationing environments while meeting fundamental human necessities become more intense.

Preservation endeavors should incorporate practical improvement techniques that address the necessities of developing populaces without compromising biodiversity. This includes advancing family arranging, supporting local area based protection drives, and executing approaches that offset preservation objectives with human prosperity.

4.2 Destitution and Unreasonable Livelihoods:

Destitution frequently drives networks to participate in exercises that hurt the climate, like unlawful logging, poaching, and horrendous rural practices. As individuals battle to meet their essential necessities, protection drives might confront obstruction or detachment.

To address this test, preservation endeavors ought to focus on destitution mitigation, perceiving the interconnectedness of social and ecological prosperity. Carrying out practical job projects, advancing eco-the travel industry, and cultivating local area based preservation models can break the pattern of destitution and natural debasement.

4.3 Absence of Admittance to Training:

Restricted admittance to training adds to unreasonable asset use and an absence of mindfulness about protection issues. Networks with low degrees of training may not completely appreciate the results of their activities on biodiversity or have the information required for reasonable asset the executives.

Protection techniques ought to incorporate instructive projects that bring issues to light about the worth of biodiversity, environment administrations, and the significance of preservation. Enabling people group with information cultivates a feeling of stewardship and empowers manageable practices.

Innovative Difficulties:

5.1 Development of Intrusive Species:

The globalization of exchange and travel works with the inadvertent acquaintance of intrusive species with new environments. Obtrusive species can outcompete local widely varied vegetation, disturb environmental cycles, and add to the decay of native species.

Successful biosecurity measures, early location and reaction frameworks, and public mindfulness crusades are critical for tending to the difficulties presented by obtrusive species. Moreover, examination and development in bother control techniques that limit natural effects are fundamental parts of preservation endeavors.

5.2 Arising Illnesses and Pandemics:

The interconnectedness of biological systems and the rising closeness among natural life and human populaces make conditions helpful for the development of zoonotic sicknesses. The Coronavirus pandemic featured the potential for infections to hop from natural life to people, with ramifications for both general wellbeing and biodiversity.

Protection endeavors should think about the wellbeing ramifications of human-untamed life associations and the potential for illness transmission. Techniques remember checking and overseeing illness flare-ups for untamed life, executing measures to decrease the gamble of transmission, and encouraging interdisciplinary cooperation among preservation and general wellbeing areas.

5.3 Innovative Dangers to Preservation Security:

The utilization of innovation by poachers and unlawful dealers represents a danger to protection security. Drones, night-vision hardware, and encoded specialized techniques engage hoodlums to dodge customary policing. The quick advancement of innovation expects moderates to remain ahead regarding reconnaissance and assurance techniques.

Creating and taking on trend setting innovations for preservation, like man-made consciousness, satellite observing, and blockchain for following natural life items, can upgrade safety efforts. Joint effort with innovation specialists and associations can guarantee the incorporation of state of the art arrangements into preservation methodologies.

Administration and Strategy Difficulties:

6.1 Shortcomings in Natural Administration:

Lacking natural administration and frail requirement of preservation arrangements thwart viable assurance of biodiversity. Debasement, absence of political will, and administrative holes add to impractical practices and the double-dealing of regular assets.

Reinforcing ecological administration includes upholding for strategy changes, upgrading legitimate structures, and cultivating straightforwardness and responsibility. Global joint effort is vital for address administration challenges that frequently rise above public limits.

6.2 International Pressures and Worldwide Disparity:

International pressures and worldwide disparities can obstruct global participation on protection issues. Abberations in monetary power, clashing public interests, and rivalry for assets might sabotage cooperative endeavors to address transboundary ecological difficulties.

Advancing tact, building agreement on shared preservation objectives, and tending to the underlying drivers of international strains are significant for beating the difficulties presented by worldwide disparity. Global associations and settlements assume an essential part in encouraging collaboration and organizing preservation drives.

6.3 Restricted Financing and Asset Allotment:

Protection endeavors frequently face difficulties connected with restricted subsidizing and asset assignment. Rivalry for monetary assets, changing political needs, and financial slumps can bring about inadequate help for basic preservation drives.

Upholding for expanded subsidizing, differentiating income streams, and encouraging public-private associations are fundamental procedures for tending to monetary requirements. Underscoring the financial advantages of protection, for example, ecotourism and environment administrations, can likewise add to getting economical subsidizing.

Social and Social Elements:

7.1 Social Mentalities Toward Natural life:

Social perspectives toward natural life fluctuate broadly, and certain conventional practices might present difficulties for preservation. Convictions in the restorative properties of specific creature parts, social practices that include the utilization of natural life items, or strict customs that influence biodiversity present obstacles for protection endeavors.

Socially delicate preservation systems include drawing in with neighborhood networks, figuring out social viewpoints, and advancing elective practices that line up with protection objectives. Cooperative methodologies that regard and integrate conventional information can work with positive change.

7.2 Changing Socioeconomics and Urbanization:

Moving socioeconomics, described by expanding urbanization and evolving ways of life, influence protection elements. Metropolitan populaces might become separated from nature, prompting diminished help for protection drives. Furthermore, changing dietary inclinations and utilization examples might drive expanded interest for asset escalated items.

Preservation procedures ought to adjust to changing socioeconomics by integrating metropolitan centered mindfulness crusades, advancing supportable metropolitan preparation, and tending to the ecological effects of urbanization. Interfacing metropolitan populaces with nature through green spaces and instructive projects is pivotal for cultivating a protection ethos.

7.3 Native Privileges and Land Residency:

The acknowledgment of native privileges and the assurance of customary land residency are fundamental parts of moral preservation. Dismissing native information and underestimating nearby networks from dynamic cycles can prompt opposition and clashes.

Preservation endeavors ought to focus on associations with native networks, regarding their privileges, and incorporating conventional environmental information into protection rehearses. Perceiving and supporting native drove protection drives adds to the drawn out progress of preservation attempts.

9.3 Strategies for Building a Sustainable Future for Tigers

The protection of tigers, superb and imperiled enormous felines, requires purposeful endeavors and key drives to guarantee a feasible future for these notorious species. As traditionalists face the difficulties of natural surroundings misfortune, poaching, and environmental change, executing viable systems is critical to defending tiger populaces around the world.

Territory Assurance and Rebuilding:

Saving and reestablishing tiger natural surroundings is central to their endurance. Laying out and keeping up with safeguarded regions, public parks, and untamed life hallways are fundamental methodologies. Legislatures, preservation associations, and nearby networks should team up to assign and protect scenes where tigers can wander unreservedly, chase, and breed. This includes resolving issues like unlawful logging, infringement, and unreasonable land-use rehearses that add to living space corruption.

Hostile to Poaching Measures and Policing:

Fortifying enemy of poaching endeavors is basic to check the unlawful natural life exchange that undermines tigers. This incorporates sending thoroughly prepared enemy of poaching units, utilizing trend setting innovations like robots and camera traps, and improving insight organizations to follow and secure poachers. Severe policing, with expanded punishments for natural life wrongdoings, goes about as an impediment and disturbs the coordinated crook networks engaged with the unlawful exchange of tiger parts.

Local area Based Protection Drives:

Drawing in neighborhood networks in tiger preservation is basic for building manageable arrangements. Local area based drives engage occupants to become stewards of their regular habitat. Executing programs that give elective vocations, schooling, and medical services mitigates neediness as well as diminishes reliance on exercises hindering to tiger environments. Cooperation with native networks, perceiving their conventional information, further reinforces the connection between preservation endeavors and neighborhood populaces.

Transboundary Joint effort:

Tigers don't stick to political lines, making transboundary joint effort fundamental for their preservation. Nations that share tiger living spaces should cooperate to lay out and keep up with interconnected scenes. Drives like the Terai Curve Scene in Nepal and India embody the advantages of cross-line cooperation. Joint endeavors work with the development of tigers across borders, guaranteeing hereditary variety and improving in general preservation results.

Environment Versatile Preservation:

As environmental change represents a developing danger to biological systems, preservation techniques should be versatile and environment strong. This includes distinguishing and safeguarding environment strong territories, as well as executing measures to assist species with adjusting to evolving conditions. Progressives need to screen the effect of environmental change on tiger living spaces, foresee expected shifts in conveyance, and foster systems to help the drawn out feasibility of populaces.

Reasonable The travel industry Practices:

Dependable ecotourism can contribute both monetarily and ecologically to tiger preservation. Overseen appropriately, the travel industry can create assets for preservation drives and bring issues to light about the significance of safeguarding tigers and their natural surroundings.

Carrying out rules for manageable the travel industry, advancing moral natural life seeing practices, and guaranteeing that neighborhood networks benefit from the travel industry exercises are fundamental for offsetting preservation with monetary interests.

Schooling and Mindfulness Missions:

Building a practical future for tigers requires a very much educated and drew out in the open. Schooling and mindfulness crusades assume a significant part in molding public discernment and gathering support for protection drives. Carrying out school programs, local area studios, and online missions that feature the significance of tigers in keeping up with biological equilibrium encourages a feeling of obligation and stewardship among people.

Hereditary Administration and Reproducing Projects:

Hereditary variety is urgent for the drawn out wellbeing and flexibility of tiger populaces. Vital reproducing programs, both in the wild and in bondage, plan to keep up with hereditary variety and forestall inbreeding. Coordinated effort among zoos, untamed life stores, and preservation associations guarantees the progress of these projects. Cautious checking of hereditary profiles and carrying out movements when vital add to the protection of solid and hereditarily assorted tiger populaces.